THE ANATOLIAN SHEPHERD AS A FAMILY DOG

Ben Smith

Publication Data

Ben Smith
The Anatolian Shepherd as a Family Dog – First edition.
Summary: "Successfully raising your Anatolian Shepherd to be the perfect family dog" – Provided by publisher.
ISBN: 978-1-954288-23-2
[1. Anatolian Shepherd – Non-Fiction] I. Title.

This book has been written with the published intent to provide accurate and author-itative information in regard to the subject matter included. While every reasonable precaution has been taken in preparation of this book the author and publisher expressly disclaim responsibility for any errors, omissions, or adverse effects arising from the use or application of the information contained inside. The techniques and suggestions are to be used at the reader's discretion and are not to be considered a substitute for professional veterinary care. If you suspect a medical problem with your dog, consult your veterinarian.

Design by Sorin Rădulescu
First hardcover edition, 2021

TABLE OF CONTENTS

CHAPTER 4

What to Have on Hand for Your Anatolian Shepherd

CHAPTER 5

Bringing Home Your Anatolian Shepherd

CHAPTER 6

Housetraining

PUBLISHER'S NOTE

Owning an Anatolian Shepherd is an experience unlike any other in the canine world. The breed is intelligent, independent, and extremely driven to protect and guard what they view as "theirs". This includes guarding property, livestock, and people, among other things.

Within these pages you will find information on almost all aspects of properly caring for and loving your ASD, including selecting, socializing, basic obedience training, nutrition, health care, and senior care. However, the training of an Anatolian Shepherd as a livestock guardian goes beyond the scope of the book you are about to read. There are already several comprehensive books on the subject that teach the nuances of training a LGD better than we ever could. These include:

Livestock Protection Dogs: Selection, Care and Training – Dawydiak and Sims

Livestock Guardians – Janet Vorwald Dohner

The Way of The Pack: Understanding and Living With Livestock Guardian Dogs – Brenda Negri

To understand the techniques, training methods, and psychology behind a working Anatolian Shepherd dog, use those books listed above. They give invaluable information that goes well beyond the depth of this book, which focuses on the non-working Anatolian, as learned from and experienced through Theo, the authors rescue ASD.

A special thanks goes out to Rachel Amov and the Anatolian Shepherd Dog Club of America (https://asdca.club/) for their collaboration and help in developing this book. Their input and advice was invaluable throughout the publishing process.

INTRODUCTION

First, let me tell you how happy I am that you are reading this book about the dog I have fallen in love with. The Anatolian Shepherd is almost impossible for me to describe and a breed that I cannot believe I had no knowledge of before one stumbled into my life. But just like the way I met my wife, I've found that the best things in life often "just happen."

Now, I am in no way a dog trainer or an expert. I'm no Caesar Milan, and I've never worked at a pet store, either. But I've been around dogs for my entire adult life, and it is through my direct experience and observations with the Anatolian Shepherd that I have come to collect valuable insight into what owning one is like. I wasn't prepared for having one in my life, and I honestly didn't think it could be that different from owning any other type of dog. I was dead wrong.

Through my experiences, work with professional trainers, discussions with owners of livestock guardian dogs, veterinarians, and many other people in the industry, I have compiled in this book the things I wish I'd known about the Anatolian Shepherd and how to best prepare for life with one. We'll look at the steps, starting from choosing your puppy all the way to caring for your elderly companion.

There's no science involved in this book. I can't tell you all the reasons why your dog loves you no matter what. I can't tell you why dogs always want to be with you and how they know when you're upset or hurt. But I can tell you exactly how to best prepare yourself and your Anatolian for a meaningful and happy life together with you and your family.

I made a lot of mistakes trying to figure out how to be my best self for my dog, Theo. I want to help you navigate past those mistakes and avoid some of the ones I made. But no matter your reason for coming across this book or your desire for an Anatolian Shepherd, just remember that your dog is a part of your life, but you are his entire life.

Ben Smith

Theo in the Snow

2

CHAPTER 1
About the Anatolian Shepherd

What is the Anatolian Shepherd?

The Anatolian Shepherd is a physical specimen. I don't mean to insinuate that the Anatolian is the biggest, fastest, or strongest dog out there, because, well, it would take you all of about ten seconds of watching Theo run around to know that the Anatolian is no Greyhound. Rather, the Anatolian is an amazing mix of size, strength, speed, and brains that borders between incredible and downright intimidating. Don't let the potentially imposing nature of this dog turn you off, however. I challenge you to find a more loyal, protective, and hardworking pup to look after you, your livestock, and your family; I'll tell you from experience that you're not going to.

Photo Courtesy of Ashley Clement

The History of the Anatolian

> *The Anatolian Shepherd breed in the US is actually a collage of different dog types from Turkey that were all used for Livestock Guardian duties. The Akbash and Karabash among them.*
>
> **PHILLIP SIMMONDS**
> *Simmonds Ranch*

The Anatolian Shepherd can be traced back centuries to ancient Babylonian times. In the mountains of Anatolia (modern-day Turkey), the ancestors of the dog, believed to be the Coban Kopegi (the name that their shepherds referred to them by), were renowned for their guardianship of livestock and for their penchant for protecting anyone and anything that was part of their flock. Other accounts trace the dog back to the ancient hunting dogs of Mesopotamia. What is known for sure is that ranchers and farmers in these regions bred the dogs over time to create a livestock guardian that could be both physically imposing and agile enough to fend off fast predators like cheetahs and wolves.

Additionally, shepherds, farmers, and ranchers wanted to produce a dog of similar size and color to their animals to allow it to blend in with their flocks. To be clear, this is not a breed of dog with a clear-cut origin story that can be pointed to as how it all began. The Anatolian Shepherd as we know it developed and was renowned in the region for its protective instinct, intimidating stature, and ability to protect large herds of livestock. Their creation lends itself to a very real human need to protect their animals and to ensure that predators would keep their distance. Shepherds in the modern-day region of Turkey needed a dog that they could trust to watch over their flock while they attended to other matters. The need to create a canine that could safeguard animals and protect lands became paramount. The Anatolian Shepherd is a prime example of how this gradual breeding produced a dog that could work independent of constant direction and make decisions on how to best protect its flock on its own.

The Anatolian was first brought to the United States during a top-secret World War II project to determine which breed was best suited to work in sheep pastures. The project ultimately concluded prematurely due to a food shortage in the United States and a desire to appease the Turks, who did not want the Americans selling their treasured breed. They were introduced back into the United States in the 1970s and recognized by the AKC in the mid-1990s, later classified in the working dog category in 1998.

The Kangal and the Anatolian Shepherd are often mistaken as being one and the same; however, that's not exactly the case. The Kangal is also native to the Anatolian region but is an extremely specific breed of livestock guardian dog. The Anatolian Shepherd is native to the Anatolian region and is widely revered for its livestock guardian abilities. It has also become more popular as of late in the United States as a nonworking companion.

Physical Characteristics

The Anatolian Shepherd is one of those dogs that looks familiar to most people, but when you say the breed name, many people are puzzled at first by what the Anatolian looks like.

When looking for an Anatolian, you'll find that this dog possesses an unmistakable beauty without sacrificing physical utility. First, touching upon the appearance, as it will be the first thing to note when seeing an adult dog and knowing what to expect when your puppy grows up, the Anatolian is large. Male height starts at 29 inches, weighing anywhere between 110-150 pounds on average, while female height starts at 27 inches tall and weighs in between 80-120 pounds. That being noted, these dogs can be smaller or larger depending on their lineage, and overall size should make for a proportionate dog. Please note: The Anatolian should never be what one would consider "fat."

The Anatolian Shepherd Dog (ASD) has a smooth face when relaxed, and their head is a large and broad one with a slight furrow down the centerline of their face. The nose and flews must be solid black. The Anatolian's eyes typically come in shades of dark brown or light amber. These eyes can often appear sad, but that's just a natural look for this dog. Medium-sized and almond-shaped, you may just find that even your full-grown Anatolian is always giving you those "puppy dog" eyes.

When your dog gets to maturity, you will be able to note its exceptionally large and powerful-looking shoulders and well-sprung ribs. Featuring long legs with a tuck up at the loin, the ASD's body has been finely tuned to allow it to remain agile while physically imposing and able to bring down predators if need be. Some have clocked the Anatolian Shepherd running at speeds up to 35 miles per hour! This amazing combination of speed and size allows it to leap and spring itself upon a predator from virtually any angle if it absolutely must.

The Anatolian's back does not have any prominent curvature, and when walking, it can resemble a large stalking predator, like a lion. Their tails can be naturally carried in two main positions, and most will vary depending on their state of attention. A relaxed dog will usually hold its tail down with a slight curve extending away from the dog's backside. The Anatolian Shepherd's tail can come in a variety of forms, so a bit of variance from dog to dog is nothing to be concerned with. A dog at attention will have a curved tail that forms a circle atop its lower back, but there is a lot of variation involved, and it is best to check the official AKC standard.

Anatolians have a double coat that is usually short or of medium length, with some variations known to exist. The coat lends itself to the ability to shed dirt that accumulates from protecting their flock and prevents matting or getting tangled.

In terms of coloration, all colors are acceptable for the Anatolian, while the most well-known and distinguishable is fawn with black ears and mask. The color variations in the ASD are not due to an attempt to make distinctions between different breeds of the dog but occur due to genetic differences. While this dog does have an AKC standard, it has never been bred for vanity.

AKC STANDARD

I have attached the Official Standard of the Anatolian Shepherd Dog from the AKC here for you to look at, as it has a lot of vital information that you should know in addition to what I have already shared above.

OFFICIAL STANDARD OF THE ANATOLIAN SHEPHERD DOG

GENERAL APPEARANCE:
Large, rugged, powerful, and impressive, possessing great endurance and agility. Developed through a set of very demanding circumstances for a purely utilitarian purpose; he is a working guard dog without equal, with a unique ability to protect livestock.

- General impression - Appears bold, but calm, unless challenged. He possesses size, good bone, a well-muscled torso with a strong head. Reserve out of its territory is acceptable. Fluid movement and even temperament is desirable.

SIZE, PROPORTION, SUBSTANCE
General balance is more important than absolute **size**. Dogs should be from 29 inches and weighing from 110 to 150 pounds proportionate to size and structure. Bitches should be from 27 inches, weighing from

80 to 120 pounds, proportionate to size and structure. Neither dog nor bitch appear fat. Both dog and bitch should be rectangular, in direct proportion to height. Measurements and weights apply at age 2 or older.

HEAD

Expression should be intelligent. Eyes are medium size, set apart, almond shaped and dark brown to light amber in color. Blue eyes or eyes of two different colors are a disqualification. Eye rims will be black or brown and without sag or looseness of haw.

Incomplete pigment is a serious fault. Ears should be set on no higher than the plane of the head. V-shaped, rounded apex, measuring about four inches at the base to six inches in length. The tip should be just long enough to reach the outside corner of the eyelid. Ears dropped to sides. Erect ears are a disqualification. Skull is large but in proportion to the body. There is a slight centerline furrow, fore and aft, from apparent stop to moderate occiput. Broader in dogs than in bitches.

Muzzle is blockier and stronger for the dog, but neither dog nor bitch would have a snipey head or muzzle. Nose and flews must be solid black or brown. Seasonal fading is not to be penalized. Incomplete pigment is a serious fault. Flews are normally dry but pronounced enough to contribute to "squaring" the overall muzzle appearance. Teeth and gums strong and healthy. Scissors bite preferred; level bite acceptable. Broken teeth are not to be faulted. Overshot, undershot or wry bite are disqualifications.

NECK, TOPLINE, BODY

Neck slightly arched, powerful, and muscular, moderate in length with more skin and fur than elsewhere on the body, forming a protective ruff. The dewlap should not be pendulous and excessive. Topline will appear level when gaiting. Back will be powerful, muscular, and level, with drop behind withers and gradual arch over loin, sloping slightly downward at the croup. Body well proportioned, functional, without exaggeration. Never fat or soft. Chest is deep (to the elbow) and well-sprung with a distinct tuck up at the loin. Tail should be long and reaching to the hocks. Set on rather high. When relaxed, it is carried low with the end curled upwards. When alert, the tail is carried high, making a "wheel." Both low and wheel carriage are acceptable when gaiting. "Wheel" carriage preferred. The tail will not necessarily uncurl totally.

FOREQUARTERS

Shoulders should be muscular and well developed, blades long, broad and sloping. Elbows should be neither in nor out. Forelegs should be relatively long, well-boned and set straight with strong pasterns. The feet are strong and compact with well-arched toes, oval in shape. They should have stout nails with pads thick and tough. Dewclaws may be removed.

HINDQUARTERS

Strong, with broad thighs and heavily muscled. Angulation at the stifle and hock are in proportion to the forequarters. As seen from behind, the legs are parallel. The feet are strong and compact with well-arched toes, oval in shape. Double dewclaws may exist. Dewclaws may be removed

COAT

Short (one inch minimum, not tight) to Rough (approximately 4 inches in length) with neck hair slightly longer. Somewhat longer and thicker at the neck and mane. A thick undercoat is common to all. Feathering may occur on the ear fringes, legs, breeching, and tail.

COLOR

All color patterns and markings are equally acceptable.

GAIT

At the trot, the gait is powerful yet fluid. When viewed from the front or rear, the legs turn neither in nor out, nor do feet cross or interfere with each other. With increased speed, footfall converges toward the center line of gravity. When viewed from the side, the front legs should reach out smoothly with no obvious pounding. The withers and back-line should stay nearly level with little rise or fall. The rear assembly should push out smoothly with hocks doing their share of the work and flexing well.

TEMPERAMENT

Alert and intelligent, calm and observant. Instinctively protective, he is courageous and highly adaptable. He is very loyal and responsive. Highly territorial, he is a natural guard. Reserve around strangers and off its territory is acceptable. Responsiveness with animation is not characteristic of the breed.

Overhandling would be discouraged.

DISQUALIFICATIONS

Blue eyes or eyes of two different colors. Erect ears. Overshot, undershot, or wry bite.

Behavioral Characteristics

Saying Anatolians are independent is putting it extremely mildly. I'm pretty confident that Theo listens to my wife and me after countless hours of training only because he's caught on to the ruse and knows a treat is coming if he plays along. The Anatolian is highly desired as a guardian due to its ability to work without human intervention and its uncanny ability to make decisions about its flock. If you are looking for a dog that will be easy to train and you can teach to roll over on command, please, keep moving, because the Anatolian is not particularly interested in doing what you would like it to do.

Theo knows many commands, and the Anatolian can be trained, but recall and consistency remain a challenge, even after hundreds of hours of diligent work. If you are seeking a strong-willed, stubborn pup that can do its job without you needing to worry, this is certainly the dog for you, but this is not a Golden Retriever-type dog. The Anatolian has been specifically bred to ensure independence and decision-making. Even if you raise the dog in the house and train it consistently, you will need to be okay with a degree of independent behavior being exhibited daily. If you are seeking a breed bred for obedience, this is not it.

It was incredibly sobering to bring Theo home and watch him grow into such a strong-willed dog. As a puppy, Anatolians are large, relative to many other dog breeds, but what we experienced was that Theo was very docile. He rarely barked, was extremely friendly, got along great with our cat (after some hesitation from our kitty), and didn't exhibit any of the possessive, guardianlike traits mentioned above. We would bring Theo to the park, where he would play with the other pups, showing off his goofy run as he navigated life as a big baby with gigantic clubs for paws. Laura and I would tell anyone that would listen how we were so lucky to have such an easygoing, friendly dog that got along great with people, dogs, and who we could take anywhere. At this point, we still had no idea what an Anatolian Shepherd was. The rescue had told us he was a medium-sized shepherd mix.

I remember vividly how Laura and I were eating out at a local restaurant in our town one day, and Theo was chomping on a bone at our feet. At this point, he was probably eight months old and still had shown none of the traits I've described about the Anatolian. Someone started to walk by our table, perhaps a bit too close, but nothing that Laura and I would think was strange. Suddenly, Theo's hackles rose, and his teeth were out, and he was barking his head off! Laura and I were dumbfounded! We tried to calm Theo, thinking that perhaps he sensed something "off" about this person, which you often hear dogs can do, but we didn't think much of it.

9

We brushed the incident off, finished our meal, and went about our day—nothing to see here, right? But what began as a seemingly innocent display of aggression turned into a shift in behavior. Theo began to bark, and "he never barks!" If the door opened to our building, he'd bark; if he saw a dog outside, he'd bark; heck, I think if a leaf blew around too close for his liking, you guessed it, he'd bark! Who was this dog, and what had he done with our Theo?

Laura began to do research into Theo, looking up information about dogs with similar physical characteristics—but

FUN FACT

Anatolian Shepherd Dog Club of America (ASDCA)

Founded in 1970, the Anatolian Shepherd Dog Club of America (ASDCA) is the American Kennel Club (AKC) Parent Club for this breed. Anatolian Shepherd Dogs were officially recognized by the AKC on June 12, 1995, and were the 144th breed to be recognized by this organization. There are more than 4,200 Anatolians registered with the ASDCA as of 2020. For more information about membership or to access the breeders' list maintained by this organization, visit their website at www.asdca.org.

not finding much. I don't remember the particulars, but our vet suggested we look up something called the Anatolian Shepherd, and when we did, it was our "aha!" moment. We began reading everything we could about this breed, convinced that this must be what Theo was. The dogs looked just like him, and lo and behold, many of the characteristics he had begun to show were indicative of a maturing Anatolian. Suddenly Theo's protectiveness over us and the fact that we couldn't take him to the dog park that he once loved any longer because he had become territorial over it all made sense.

Is the Anatolian Shepherd Right for Me?

So, the question that you must ask yourself is if the Anatolian is what you need in your life. They're big and adorable, yes, but they are also working dogs. If you're looking for them to work for you, they absolutely will and better than any other dog. But if you're looking for just a companion, you really, really need to consider your options because the Anatolian is a breed that is not content to follow orders and needs a domain to preside over. I certainly do not recommend this type of dog to the first-time owner or to the inexperienced.

Luckily, Laura had owned a big dog before she and I met, but Theo is my first dog, and I cannot imagine two first-time dog owners trying to learn how

Photo Courtesy of Chris and Shannon Haggard

to manage an Anatolian. However, if enough studying is done and resources are utilized, it may be possible for the right people or person. Anyone with Anatolians will tell you that although this breed is unlike any other dog you will have ever come across, and owning one is the most rewarding of experiences, it is not for everyone.

THE BIG DOG STIGMA

You must prepare yourself for some nasty looks and for your dog to be treated with the very unfair "big dog" stigma that German Shepherds, Pit Bulls, Rottweilers, and Dobermans receive. Of course, if you've got a well-behaved dog, those nasty looks should be minimal, but any step out of line will generate these looks, even the slightest! Although studies have shown that the three most "aggressive" dog breeds are all small breed dogs, the imposing stature of a big dog with its loud bark will draw plenty of unwanted attention to you both. Make sure that your dog grows comfortable on the leash when you walk around, and make sure that you understand that discipline and love are very intertwined, and proper discipline is as much about love as anything else. Discipline will be especially important with a large and powerful breed like the Anatolian. There's a time and place for affection, but your dog has to know who is in charge, especially in public.

POTENTIAL HEALTH CONCERNS

While the Anatolian is a generally healthy dog with a long life span for a bigger breed, the ASDCA recommends hip and elbow x-rays. However, the breed is not at any higher risk for the health issues common to large breed dogs, such as hypertrophic osteodystrophy and osteochondritis dissecans.

DO YOU HAVE CHILDREN?

Anatolians can make for great family dogs. As they are naturally protective, they can make for the perfect guard dog and companion all in one. Their size makes them prone to knocking over smaller children inadvertently, so training needs to be done as early as possible and remain consistent to ensure there are no unnecessary incidents at home. If you have older children, there isn't much to worry about as the Anatolian can engage with them in playful activities that will not hurt a larger child. A word of caution would be that the Anatolian may perceive any type of "roughhousing" between your children and their friends as a threat and react accordingly. It is best to never leave your Anatolian alone with children of any age.

The true key to having an Anatolian as a family dog is understanding that if you have young children, supplying the constant training and attention necessary to properly raise and supervise your Anatolian while doing the same for your children is paramount. Understand that your dog will be full-sized well before your toddler is able to prevent itself from being knocked down by the dog. While the Anatolian is not going to be aggressive towards your child if properly socialized, always supervise your small children when they are around and playing with the dog to be on the safe side. They really are gentle, but they are giants!

TIME

Do you have the time to devote to the exercise that your (ASD) is going to require? Although these dogs do not need hours and hours of physical stimulation, they will need some land to preside over and at least 2-3 good-sized walks per day. It's a commitment; there's no other way to put it.

FUN FACT
US Federal Project Gone Awry

Some of the earliest Anatolian Shepherds to be introduced in the United States were a gift in the 1930s from the Turkish prime minister to the Secretary of Agriculture, who was Henry A. Wallace at the time. Wool was a valuable commodity during this time, and Wallace had embarked on a federal "Sheepdog Project" to determine the best sheepdog for protecting this resource. The Turkish prime minister suggested the Anatolian Shepherd and sent a pair of dogs to America. One of these dogs was pregnant when she arrived and soon gave birth to 12 puppies, which was more than the Depression-era federal government could afford to take care of. The 14 dogs were sold to a buyer in the Virgin Islands, and Wallace's project was eventually scrapped.

It's not like winding a clock and letting it tick. You need to be up for walking around in the rain, snow, sleet, and sun. With all that harsh weather walking, you also need to be ready to give baths, apply flea and tick medicines, trim nails, look for ticks, and of course, give lots of belly rubs for all the scary squirrels your ASD will drive away!

SOCIALIZATION AND PUPPY TRAINING

Take advantage of puppy classes offered by a local trainer—ideally, one that is familiar with the breed or that is good with large breed dogs. Your puppy needs to understand some basic commands and have some socialization, as discussed in detail in a later chapter. Puppy classes are the perfect venue to get this early exposure. Your Anatolian is going to be headstrong as is, so start early and be persistent; it will pay off in the end.

EXPENSES

Big dogs are more expensive due to potential health risks, appetite, and higher insurance fees. I will get into specific costs in a later chapter, but for now, just be aware that this is an investment that will likely cost over two thousand dollars a year. Don't worry, though; it'll be one of the best investments you can make.

Laura and I often joke that if we had known that Theo was an Anatolian prior to adopting him, he would have checked every box for what we were not looking for in a dog. Knowing what we now know, we wouldn't want any other pup in our household, but it has been a test of our will and of our personal relationship. Owning Theo has been the most incredible journey in our lives together, but it has been anything but easy. If you have read this chapter and have come to the clear conclusion that this is the one dog that will suit your needs, then that is amazing. But if you're getting to this point and have some doubts, then please do yourself and the pup a favor, and think about it until your doubts are gone, or pass on the Anatolian altogether.

CHAPTER 2
Choosing an Anatolian Shepherd

> "
>
> *The Anatolian Shepherd is intelligent and independent and is only suitable for an experienced owner that can earn the dog's respect. The Anatolian Shepherd has strong guardian instincts that should be employed protecting livestock or family members. The breed requires daily vigorous exercise and is best suited to large properties of 5 acres or larger. ASDs bark loudly so are not good with neighbors who expect quiet.*
>
> NANCY BURNS
> *Marble Peaks Ranch*
>
> "

It is especially important to keep in mind that a purebred Anatolian is a different type of dog than one that is even slightly mixed or otherwise less than 100% Anatolian. Anatolians are renowned for their ability to be trained for livestock guardianship and their instinct to protect, but they do need to be trained and given direction. So please remember this—I keep bringing it up for a very good reason—many Anatolians that are a few years old end up needing to be rehomed because people didn't understand the dog. There are some terrific Anatolian breeders who rehome dogs that are certainly worth looking into.

Companionship vs. Working Dog

The Anatolian is a unique dog in that its versatility as a companion versus strictly serving as a working dog can depend on who you ask and on an individual's experience. From interviews I have conducted with owners of Anatolians, most agree that the dog is incredibly versatile and can serve as

your companion, as a working dog, or as both. In the mountains of Turkey, it has been common for the dogs to be at work all day and then come down into the village if their flock did so. If you are seeking an ASD to serve in either of these roles, understand that the dog needs direction, guidance, and training. That said, if you are looking for a dog to look at you for commands, this is not that dog. Think of having a copilot as opposed to a passenger; that's the best I can do in regard to giving you an analogy for what it's like living with an Anatolian.

16

Buying vs. Rescuing

There is something very satisfying about adopting or rescuing a dog. After all, they were dumped and needed a home, whether a puppy or a more mature dog. Tens of thousands of dogs are surrendered or abandoned around the country every year. It's truly a tragedy, and it's only human to want to do something about it. That's how we ended up with Theo. Laura saw a posting online about a litter of puppies found on the side of the road in Mississippi, saw the pup that would become our Theo, said, "Oh my god, how cute!" The rest is history. I'm not saying that this isn't the way you should go about finding your potential Anatolian, but it may not be the route if you are looking for a prime example of an Anatolian. There are so many amazing Anatolian breeders out there with some of the best ASDs you'll ever come across.

Finding and Selecting a Reputable Breeder

> 66
>
> *The most important issue is knowing your purpose for owning an Anatolian Shepherd, and finding a breeder who raises ASDs for that purpose. A dog from a show breeder does not belong guarding livestock and vice versa. An experienced breeder knows there are differences in temperament between breeding lines and even within litters. Some Anatolian Shepherds are very aloof and aggressive and should work on large ranches with significant threat of predation. Some are very human-oriented and work well protecting children. Many people mistakenly believe that a dog from champion lines must be the "best" when in fact show champions are chosen primarily on conformation and gait. Always ask the breeder for OFA results for hip and elbow dysplasia and whether they know of other genetic problems in their lines such as entropion or seizure disorders.*
>
> NANCY BURNS
> *Marble Peaks Ranch*
> 99

Finding a reputable breeder is critical if you are looking for a working Anatolian to protect your livestock. Ensuring that you are buying an Anatolian with the right temperament, right socialization, and with the proper health tests done is an essential part of bringing an ASD home. For a list of reputable breeders, check out the ASDCA website (http://www.asdca.org/). When rescuing a dog, you get what you get, so to speak. There can be several different bloodlines going into that dog that have altered its instincts and desire to do work and, perhaps, have even made it unsuitable for the type of jobs you envision it doing. This can be the case even if it looks like an Anatolian Shepherd. When it comes to looking for a working dog, you really need to do your homework and ensure that you are in contact with a reputable breeder.

HOW TO FIND A REPUTABLE BREEDER

There are several ways to find a reputable Anatolian Shepherd Breeder. My recommendation is to do a lot of background work on any breeder you come across on the internet. The more information that they have on a webpage, the better. At the absolute minimum, their sires and dams, their personal experience with the dogs, what their goals are for the puppies, and any other information like AKC status should be displayed publicly.

Now, how do you know what to look for when you approach a breeder? This can be tricky as databases that list reputable breeders tend to be a bit slow when it comes to updating. This means that any breeder can theoretically add themselves to a database, check off whichever boxes they want to represent themselves with, and it may not be verified before the public can view their listing on the UKC or AKC website or on other sites. So, it is particularly important to look up a dog by their registration number, and you should be able to look up the sire (father) and dam (mother) of a purebred dog through the UKC or AKC website as well. Again, visiting the ASDCA website and looking through their breeder's list is an absolute must.

QUESTIONS TO ASK IN A PHONE INTERVIEW

Prior to heading on-site to look at the puppies and parents, you should get comfortable with the idea of having a detailed discussion with the breeder about their puppies. Some questions you should ask:

- Ask if the parents will be available to meet during a visit. This will give you a great idea of what any puppy you purchase may eventually turn into regarding size, temperament, and looks. All of these are important to take into consideration.

- Have health tests been performed on the parents? Many people remember to ask about the puppy's tests, but fewer think to ask about the tests the parents have undergone.

- How long have you been breeding the Anatolian Shepherd? What is your experience with this breed? Due to the uniqueness of the Anatolian, it is good to know how long the breeder has been in business and how familiar they are with the Anatolian. You really do not want anything less than an expert with this dog. They should be knowledgeable about the breed's strengths and weaknesses and any genetic diseases that might affect their breed. Ask about any clubs the breeder may be a part of and/or any activities, too.

- How do you socialize your puppies/do you engage the puppies in early neurological stimulation? Knowing how the puppy is around other dogs is crucial to understanding how it is going to develop. Puppies should not be unusually shy or scared, so finding out what the breeder does to prevent these traits is crucial.

- How do you determine if a puppy will be a working or show dog? The best Anatolian breeders can determine the type of animals that the puppy will be best at working with or if the dog is meant to be a show dog. A good breeder knows their breed intimately and can gain a detailed sense of a dog's strengths and weaknesses early on. You want to arm yourself with that information.

- Are vaccinations up to date? This will allow you to know exactly where the puppy is on their shot schedule and help you transition them to your veterinarian.

- How long until I can take the puppy home? Although common knowledge in the dog world, some don't know that a dog needs to stay with its mother and littermates for eight to twelve weeks to properly mature.

- What do you require from me to purchase a puppy? It's always good to know what the breeder expects of those who are attempting to purchase their dogs. They should ask you many questions, and this is a sign of a competent and trustworthy breeder who cares about the dogs they are breeding.

- How can I contact you down the road? Your breeder will be a resource for you throughout your dog's life. Knowing the best ways to reach out to them when you have questions is essential, and any trustworthy breeder should welcome those discussions.

- Finding a breeder that is trustworthy, knowledgeable, respected, and breeds excellent dogs can be a challenge. Throw in the fact that Anatolian Shepherd's are not a dog that is in abundance, it is important to practice due diligence to ensure you are working with a reputable breeder who has the dog's best interest in mind.

WHAT TO LOOK FOR ON-SITE

Be sure to examine the environment that the dogs are living in. The homelife and setting that the breeder is showing can tell you a lot about their professionalism and their overall credibility. Look at as many of the puppies as you can to examine them to get a sense of their overall temperament and health, but don't be surprised if your breeder does not allow this. The best breeders will often pick the puppy that is best for the prospective owners based on a variety of factors. Ask as many questions as you can think of, and anticipate questions being asked of you. At a minimum, the dam should be on-premise for you to look at and meet. If you are finding that there are no registration numbers or the breeder you have approached is not able to furnish this information, you are likely dealing with a scammer of some sort.

Photo Courtesy of Rachel Amov

Welcome those questions! A reputable breeder should have a desire to send their dogs to a great home. It should raise numerous red flags if the breeder seems to be unconcerned with you on a personal level and seems focused on selling the dog above all else.

Contracts

When purchasing from a breeder, there absolutely must be written contracts signed by all interested parties. Although any legal document can be intimidating when you sit down to sign it, think of the breeding contract as an assurance of all that you are guaranteed and a way for the breeder to reiterate everything they've told you already. Additionally, the contract will contain the dog's AKC registration number, the sire and dam's AKC registration numbers, and obviously the purchase price. All breeder contracts vary with the individual, but here are some other things you should expect, as well.

- The contract can outline your breeder's stance on spaying or neutering your pet. Some breeders believe it is best to spay and neuter when a dog has finished maturing and the growth plates have closed, which can be around 18 months for Anatolians. It is best to know your veterinarian's stance so that there are no conflicts to mitigate later on.

- If you plan on entering your dog at AKC events, ensure that you have full registration and not just limited registration. The registered name of your dog will be used, which is different from the name you call your dog at home. Some breeders can be very specific about what the registration name must be on the dog for the AKC paperwork, so it is best to read this section carefully and discuss with your breeder what their expectation is for the dog's official AKC name.

FUN FACT

National Anatolian Shepherd Rescue Network (NASRN)

The National Anatolian Shepherd Rescue Network (NASRN) is an all-volunteer-run 501(c)(3) nonprofit that works with shelters around America that are attempting to rehome Anatolian Shepherds. The volunteer team is primarily comprised of Anatolian Shepherd owners who also offer assistance to others who may be struggling with behavioral issues. For more information about this organization and to view available dogs, visit www.nasrn.com.

- Return-to-Breeder clauses are standard in reputable breeders' contracts. If something goes wrong, and you cannot take care of the dog any longer, the breeder usually possesses the right to first refusal. Most breeder's contracts will contain this clause, and most breeders will want to take the dog from you, or at a minimum, be able to help with the rehoming process. They have poured their life into providing loving homes to these dogs, and most want to impart the same knowledge they gave to you to ensure that the dog is getting the care that they need from a loving home.

There is a tremendous amount of variance when it comes to breeder contracts. Occasionally you will find things that you either are confused by or simply do not agree to. It is always best to sit down with your breeder and go through the contract line by line and discuss things that you have any concerns over. You should never enter into a legal contract that you either don't understand or agree with or that you do not plan on honoring. It is not good for you, the breeder, or the puppy.

Health Checks the Breeder Should Perform

With a purebred Anatolian, it is particularly important to know that the breeder has had the dog's hips and elbows tested for dysplasia. Prospective owners can visit the Orthopedic Foundation for Animals website (https://www.ofa.org) to search the dog to verify their ratings in various health areas, too.

It is important to know your breeder's stance on returns. Whether you find a defect after taking the dog home or if it is just simply not working out, it is important to find a breeder who is willing to take a dog back. The contract that you each sign needs to include obligations for both parties and a health guarantee from the breeder. Do not take anyone's word; have them put it in writing.

Rescuing an Anatolian

Now, when it comes to rescuing an Anatolian Shepherd, it is not that you won't have any luck finding a purebred Anatolian up for adoption. However, there is really no way of knowing that that is what you are receiving without a breeder who has done the proper testing, which is generally not the case at rescues, although Red Mountain Mutts in Central California and the National Anatolian Shepherd Rescue Network do tremendous work in this area. The Anatolian Shepherd can be mixed with several different dogs, and a dog that looks purebred might not be a purebred ASD. It is best to consult with experts at the NASRN, as they possess the breed expertise to ensure you are getting a purebred Anatolian instead of a mix. Additionally, purebred Anatolian puppies are extremely rare, and if a shelter or rescue has them, they will often be mislabeled as a shepherd mix due to a lack of knowledge of the mere existence of the breed.

HOW TO FIND A GOOD PLACE TO RESCUE AN ANATOLIAN

Stay away from malls or any place that cannot provide you with some sort of paperwork that specifies where the dog/puppy came from. Mall pet stores are notorious for bringing in dogs from puppy mills. I have two sure-fire resources to help you find an Anatolian for adoption: the official ASDCA Rescue and the previously mentioned National Anatolian Shepherd Rescue Network. If you are concerned about puppy mills and want to steer clear of them at all costs (you should), reach out to either organization, and they will help you with every question that you have—seriously. These people have been in the business for years, and they dedicate themselves to public education about the Anatolian and helping find homes for Anatolians who have been put up for adoption.

Look, this is not a golden retriever. Anatolians will take your commands, but they may or may not follow them due to their independent thinking traits. This is a very specific breed of dog and still isn't particularly popular or well-known in the United States. So simply asking a shelter if they have any will likely provide little to no help. I've called many shelters and spoken to people well-known in the Anatolian world, and I've gathered this much: Anatolian Shepherds are usually lumped in as a "shepherd mix" by over 90% of shelters across the nation due to a lack of breed awareness. This isn't because a shelter is low-quality or not doing its job; the reality is that the Anatolian Shepherd is a dog that is not popular in this country, as they do not make for great pets in the traditional sense.

But luckily for you, the NASRN exists. They work together with shelters across the country to help rehome dogs and provide fosters to purebred and crossbred Anatolians who need loving homes. And perhaps most importantly of all, they genuinely love the ASD and are extremely specific about who they will allow to adopt these dogs. Don't think of this as intimidating, although it can be. Think about how much these people love these dogs to only want the best homes to be able to have them. They will provide home checks before any adoption, so they know what type of property you have. Since this breed needs space to be taken care of properly, candidates typically need to have some space for their dog to roam and proper fencing.

QUESTIONS THEY WILL ASK

When looking to adopt an Anatolian Shepherd, expect several questions to be asked of you. Do you have large dog experience? What is your pet history, and do you have pets currently? They will ask how your current pets are with other dogs and what your vet history is like. A diligent and reputable rescue likes to know if the person they are adopting out to has a history of taking care of their animals properly. You will be asked how much property you have, making sure you have the land required to properly care for an Anatolian. A responsible and knowledgeable breeder or rescue cannot, in good faith, allow an adopter with no land to take home an Anatolian Shepherd. The rescue will ensure that any outdoor spaces you have are adequately fenced with at least a 6-foot physical fence, and a knowledgeable breeder will not sell a puppy to a new owner if the fence is not up to standard.

Remember, these dogs are determined when focused. While an electric fence might contain some, it would be a big dice-roll for a reputable rescue to allow an ASD to go to a home if that was all they had. These dogs are known to go through electric fences if they become fixated on something. Shelters, breeders, and rescues may not ask these questions, but it is important that you do your due diligence and bring them up.

QUESTIONS YOU NEED TO ASK

Remember, when seeking an Anatolian to adopt or rescue, you're not usually dealing with puppies. These dogs are usually six months or older. Some helpful questions you should ask include, what is the dog's demeanor? Are they good with kids and/or other pets? If they are six months or older, their personality is starting to come out, and the "puppiness" is going away. Age is a huge factor in the demeanor and behavior that a dog exhibits. Also, keep in mind that rescues may not know some of this information or may not be completely honest with you. Do they have a high prey drive (Anatolians generally have a low prey drive, but it's worth asking)? How active are they, and how big are they expected to get? If not in the description, ask why they are up for adoption? The more you know about the dog you are looking to adopt, the better.

If a shelter does not have an answer to a vital question, apply some pressure for them to get those answers. Keep in mind the "3-3-3" rule. After three days, a dog may be weary in its new home and appear scared and have little to no appetite. After three weeks, a dog usually has become more comfortable and is getting used to the idea of being in this new place for the long haul. This may be when behavioral issues begin to show up, too. At three months, a dog is usually comfortable in its surroundings and has likely fallen into its new routine with its new family.

Laura and I happened to stumble upon a purebred Anatolian puppy when we weren't even looking for one, but this should be taken as the exception and not the rule. If you have no aversion to the breed's characteristics at this point and are willing to work awfully hard at training, then finding a reputable breeder or seeking to adopt are both great options. If you are seeking a purebred Anatolian puppy to become a working dog or perhaps to even just have a purebred Anatolian, which is not uncommon, you are best advised to find a reputable breeder who can supply you with all the information I have advised above. Unfortunately, not every breeder is looking out for the dog or the customer, and you need to request health tests, proof of lineage, and any other genetic information to be certain that you are receiving a purebred Anatolian. You're not being annoying, you're being responsible, and that is very important to remember. Reputable and responsible Anatolian breeders are more common than not, and they have the best interest of the dogs in mind. You may be less likely to find a pure ASD via adoption or rescue, but it is not impossible.

MAKING YOUR DECISION

Whether buying or adopting, owning an Anatolian is a rewarding experience for someone with the right information and mindset. Be certain that you have an opportunity to interact with the dog prior to adoption or purchase, but if you do not have the opportunity to do so, things can work out, especially if you are purchasing from a reputable breeder. It may be best, as a first-time owner, to really do your best to get out and interact with the puppy, however. Laura and I adopted sight unseen, and although it worked out for us, there are countless horror stories that point to how important it is to pick the right dog for your needs! You must consider how much land you have, if you have children, and the type of home you can provide to come to the best decision possible for you and your new dog.

CHAPTER 3

Preparing Your Home & Property for Your Anatolian Shepherd

The versatility of the Anatolian Shepherd lends itself to some intense preparation to properly create a home environment that suits the breed's need for space and mental and physical stimulation. There are necessary steps and precautions to take to ensure that you are prepared and that your home and property are ready for your new four-legged accomplice.

The Importance of Having a Plan

You've thought about your indoor and outdoor space, as well as how to introduce your dog to your other pets. Those make for a great start, but you need to have a plan for your new companion to thrive in its new environment. You certainly do not want to fly by the seat of your pants when bringing home an ASD. These dogs require discipline and clear direction, and they will sense, even as puppies, if they can get away with things around your house and property. It is incredibly important to know where you will stand on indoor and outdoor restrictions regarding where he may go, whether he will be sleeping in a crate (I STRONGLY recommend this and will discuss it in detail in chapter 6), what type of foods he will be eating, and what toys you will have around to keep your new Anatolian engaged and occupied.

You must know exactly what your dog's role is going to be in your household and on your property. Remember, you have a working dog on your hands. Even if you do not have them supervising and guarding any livestock, they will be guarding you, your property, and perhaps everything that their senses detect. Training, discipline, and repetition need to be pillars of your plan. If your dog is going to be your companion and mainly an indoor

27

dog, training, discipline, and repetition need to be pillars of your plan. See what I did there?

While the setting and role that your pup will be filling will vary greatly with your circumstance, the central tenets to having a thriving relationship and life with your ASD revolve around those core principles. Love is a big part of it, too; do not get me wrong. But if you have a well-trained and disciplined dog, it will love you like no other.

Dangerous Things Your Dog Might Eat Inside

Stay far away from grapes (they can cause kidney failure), onions, garlic, and chocolate, as those are the big-ticket items that are the most notorious for causing illnesses in canines. However, certain other items are to be avoided as well, including almonds, macadamia nuts, and ice cream. NSAID gels can also be a serious danger to dogs, too. In general, dairy can be acceptable for dogs (stay away from ice cream due to high dairy and sugar content) in small quantities. Still, it is best to avoid giving your dog large quantities as it can be difficult for canines to digest dairy. Dogs are, after all, lactose intolerant, and while small amounts of dairy are known to be acceptable, anything beyond this is not advisable.

Limit Access to Household Items

Luckily, Theo has never had a desire to chew on shoes. But when he was a puppy, he loved to chew on wires. It is easy to get frustrated at your pup for chewing things he's not supposed to, but it is ultimately your responsibility to protect your dog and your belongings. That means tucking wires, shoes, and clothing away and making sure that small items that can be ingested are off the ground and off surfaces that the Anatolian can reach (pretty much everywhere).

Make sure that your trash bins are out of reach, whether inside or outside, and understand that no precaution is too much.

Indoor Preparation

It is so important to establish rules for your Anatolian to abide by while indoors. Whether your dog will be spending most of its time inside or coming in after a day's work, you are going to want to establish boundaries and reinforce the behaviors you would like to see them exhibit repeatedly.

In our home, we have a dedicated spot for Theo's bed. This spot is close enough to where Laura and I tend to relax after a day's work but also provides a view of the entire first floor of our home so that Theo can satisfy his natural curiosity. If you choose to allow your dog on the furniture, that is your call, but if you wish to keep them off, that needs to start as soon as possible, as an Anatolian's habits will be hard to break in the future.

Make sure anything that is chewable and potentially dangerous for your dog is tucked away and out of reach. Whether you have an adult dog or just a puppy, they are driven by curiosity, and as soon as they have been in an area long enough, they will have the feeling that the space and everything in it is theirs. So, if you do not want to replace wires, chargers, shoes, or anything else, make sure it is out of sight and that your dog knows right away that it is not theirs to interact with.

If you tend to have quite a bit of clutter lying around, it is best for you to clean up as your Anatolian is going to be very, let's just say, "curious" about all of your things. They are not shy about poking around your purses, bags, boxes, and anything else you may have lying around for them to investigate. Think about the height of your counters and tables. If you're bringing home a pup, you need to keep in mind that he will one day be tall and have the ability to rest his chin on your dining room table or help himself to what is on your kitchen counters.

Outdoor Preparation

> *The Anatolian Shepherd thrives in the outdoors and needs sturdy fencing. This breed can easily chew through nylon leads, rope, and wood and pass through invisible electric fences. Woven wire, welded wire, or chain link is needed to contain ASDs from day one. Select sturdy chew toys such as firm rubber and natural raw bones and avoid fabric toys.*
>
> NANCY BURNS
> *Marble Peaks Ranch*

Adequate fencing, at least 8 feet tall, is a must for your property if you plan to have your Anatolian spend any time outdoors, supervised or not. These dogs will jump higher than you can imagine, and if they see something that grabs their attention, they can easily get over a fence of 6 feet or lower. Anatolians also love to dig, so make sure that there is no possible way they can dig underneath the fence and get themselves into trouble. This may prove difficult depending on height restrictions on fencing where you live, so having a backup electric fence would also be advisable here.

Speaking with many Anatolian owners will leave you with conflicting conclusions about the effectiveness of an electric fence. Many, many owners will tell you that the Anatolian is a very determined and focused dog and that if something grabs their attention, they will be more than willing to force their way through the electric fence to go after whatever it was that they saw. The real problem is that once they look to come back into your enclosure, they will be unable to recross the threshold to get in. Although some owners have had success with an electric fence, it is the consensus of numerous Anatolian owners' that a traditional fence is best, and if you really need to have an electric fence, make sure you have a physical fence as well.

It is wise to have plenty of water around for your pup, especially if you will be keeping him outdoors for long stretches of time. Many Anatolian owners do have their dogs come inside at night after the workday, but others will have a designated outdoor area that is insulated for their dog to sleep. Do not be alarmed if your Anatolian shuns your cozy doghouse and instead wants to sleep in the most uncomfortable places you can imagine. Anatolians are at times bizarre, aloof creatures who would rather sleep amongst their flock than on a cozy bed.

Dangerous Things That Your Dog Might Eat Outside

Your outdoor space will likely contain some type of weeds or other plant life that will seem to be a great snack for your Anatolian but could very well be toxic! If your dog is a working dog, you may have fertilizers or pesticides being sprayed in and around your property. Make sure your dog is trained from an early age to not nibble on the grass, although this will likely be impossible! If you have flowers, do extensive research as to which are toxic to your pup and which are not. Tulips and rhododendrons are extremely toxic to dogs and must be avoided!

The key takeaway is to limit the exposure of your dog to chemicals and toxic plant life that it may encounter on a farm or general outdoor area. Bored dogs with little direction will snack, just like bored humans will snack. Bored dogs will also look to escape your property! Mental stimulation in the form of a work task is a great way to keep them focused on things other than what they can eat and where else they should go. Physical and mental health will always go hand in hand!

Introducing Your Anatolian to Children

I'd recommend that you discuss with your children exactly what they would like in a dog and explain that an Anatolian Shepherd isn't a dog that they're going to be able to play with like they would a Golden Retriever. If you are adopting or purchasing an Anatolian as a family companion, it's important for your children to know about the breed's temperament and characteristics. In other words, make sure they know they're not getting a golden retriever and are instead going to get an extremely loyal but fiercely independent puppy. If your children are young, show them pictures of Anatolian puppies and get them comfortable with the idea that these

FUN FACT
Biblical Reference

Anatolian Shepherds have a rich and ancient history dating back thousands of years. One of the first written descriptions of these dogs is believed to be in the Old Testament of the Christian Bible. The Book of Job describes large dogs in amongst Job's flocks. Archeological evidence supports the theory that these were early Anatolian Shepherd Dogs. This breed is still used as sheepdogs in rural areas of Turkey today!

are larger dogs. Kids can be disappointed when they think they're getting a puppy, only to see a 40-pound "imposter" brought home.

A big key is simply communication. If your children understand the breed and what to expect, it will only be a matter of introducing your puppy to them that will require your effort and emotional focus. Your puppy will generally be curious—as will your child. Make sure that your kids know what the family goals are regarding proper socialization so that they aren't too rough with the puppy. Depending on how young your children are, they may see your new pup as more of an adult dog since your Anatolian will be larger than what your kids are likely used to seeing. Remind them that no matter the size, he's still a puppy and needs to be treated very gently. If you'd like some more pointers, refer back to chapter one.

Preparing Your Other Pets for Your Anatolian

Bringing home a dog is a time of excitement for your children. The excitement that is felt by kids is equally as stressful for any other pets you may have at home. Hopefully, you do not subscribe to the idea that you can just force your previous pets into a room with your new pet and let them "figure it out." I will tell you right now that is a huge and potentially lethal mistake to make with an Anatolian. Older Anatolians often need to be the only dog in the household, as well. It is one thing to introduce a puppy to other animals, but adult Anatolians are livestock guardians and may very likely view other animals as a threat.

The key to properly introducing your pets is a gradual process where there are physical barriers between the animals. It is entirely likely that there is going to be an adjustment period for up to a few months. This is to be expected, and ultimately, if you are patient, your new dog and previous pets will get along great. For the sake of keeping things brief, a discussion of how to introduce your dog to livestock will be in a future section.

Dogs

Depending on the type of dog(s) you have, you may wish to introduce them outside of the house prior to bringing your Anatolian indoors into your dogs' domain. To prevent any sort of shock or stressful scenario for any of the dogs, I recommend having them meet in a more neutral setting where they can get accustomed to seeing each other and being around one another. Think about having them meet in an outdoor setting that neither dog has a connection to—a neighbor's property that your older dog(s) is unfamiliar with or another setting that will ensure no territorial claims from either animal. It's important to avoid meeting at a local park due to concerns over disease transmission. Equally as important is ensuring you don't attempt this in a setting with a third dog present. You want the dogs to be alert of one another but not on alert due to the presence of others.

Think about having a familiar toy or bone for your older dog to keep them engaged and a toy for the puppy, as well. Just be careful that you don't use too high a value of toy or bone, as you don't want any fights to break out. Allowing both to "be themselves" while in each other's presence will go a long way. Be sure to keep the dogs separated for a time in the house, with each having their own area to be away from the other. This will make their bonding experience that much steadier.

Potential negative body language that you should watch out for, particularly from the older dog, are raised hackles, curling of the lip into a snarl, or the tail going in between the legs. Barking doesn't mean aggression, and that's important to note here. But you also know your dog better than anyone else, and if your dog barking usually precedes some type of aggression, it would be best to redirect their behavior and attention elsewhere.

Sniffing, circling, and licking are all positive signs that the dogs are getting acclimated to one another. A bow from either of the dogs is a sign of playfulness, and if the elder dog starts to hop around in a playful manner, that typically is an invite to the puppy to play. While it is up to you whether you'd like the two to play, keep in mind that your puppy may not be comfortable yet, even if your older dog is. Sometimes people make the mistake of believing their puppy will always want to play, and the older dog will need convincing, but that's only sometimes the case.

Cats

Laura and I had a one-year-old cat when we brought a three-month-old Anatolian into the mix. The rescue that we received Theo from had informed us that he had been around cats and was comfortable with them, so we did not have worries about how he would be around Ozzie. What we did not anticipate was how skeptical Ozzie would be of Theo. Dogs are quite territorial but multiply that significantly with a cat. Our house had always belonged to Ozzie, and it now seemed that he had a giant challenger to deal with.

Photo Courtesy of Heidi Krol Stonecoat Farm Anatolians

We took all the necessary precautions that we had learned about. We kept them separate, feeding one of them on one side of the door while the other ate on the opposite side. We introduced each of their scents to the other gradually. Ozzie always sleeps on a blanket, so we put that blanket near Theo so he'd become accustomed to the smell and get used to it. We were careful to ease them into being in the same spaces together, and they were never unsupervised. Theo still has no concept of how large he really is, and he could easily have put himself on top of Ozzie and crushed him!

Smaller Animal Introductions

So, let's say you have a pet rat or reptile or a guinea pig. Can your Anatolian Shepherd coexist with these types of pets too? The answer, in its beautiful vagueness, is that it depends. You will need to acclimate them and allow them to become comfortable with one another, and never leave them unsupervised. Even after you have acclimated the animals and it appears they get along great, **do not** leave them unsupervised and in the open together. It's just not worth it.

CHAPTER 4

What to Have on Hand for Your Anatolian Shepherd

You've made the decision! One way or another, you will be welcoming an Anatolian Shepherd into your life and are now wondering what the next steps look like. As outlined in the last chapter, there are so many precautions and preparations to make prior to bringing home your ASD. Similarly, there are many other things that you should know and be aware of to make the transition as smooth as possible.

Luckily for me, my wife is a bit of a crazy "dog mom." I say that out of love, of course. Laura wanted to make sure that Theo would feel right at home with us from the jump. Here are a few things I recommend that you have for your ASD BEFORE you bring it into your home.

The Right-Sized Crate

Dogs are territorial and enjoy a nice den. You will probably need more than one crate throughout your dog's life if you plan on having them crated even as an adult. Contrary to what might seem like common sense, less is more with a crate. Obviously, you don't want your pup to be smushed, but he doesn't need a sprawling crate that a full-grown Great Dane could fit in, either. Be sure that you are providing a crate with enough room for your puppy to sleep, stand up, and turn around in, but not so much room that he can create chaos. As I said above, I recommend crating your ASD. If left unsupervised, he will absolutely find something to get into. Do not leave your untrained puppy unsupervised, ever. This is for your own good and for your dog's. In fact, don't leave your trained puppy unsupervised, either, if you can help it.

Pads

If you're bringing home a puppy, there will be accidents. Make sure that you have pads around your home so that you can spare yourself (and any carpets) rigorous cleaning. While one-time use pads may seem to be the most convenient and practical option, they may actually be encouraging your dog to go to the bathroom indoors due to the scents that they emit. For this reason, consider using washable pads for your pup when house training, even the human kind will do. While you are trying to housetrain your pup, the pads will be mighty useful. Put a pad in each room that the dog can

access, and put a pad in your Anatolian's crate for good measure. Dogs will generally only go to the bathroom in their crate as an absolute last resort, but be mindful that puppies can be unpredictable with their potty training.

Leash and Collar

Whatever you do, DO NOT buy a retractable leash. They are dangerous, and your ASD is certainly not the kind of dog to keep on a retractable leash. With the power and force that they can launch themselves with if they so desire, you need a solid 1-2-inch-wide leash that will provide you with as much control as needed. There will come a time when your lovable puppy becomes an extremely protective adult, and you will need to be confident in your abilities to control him on the leash.

Puppy Theo had a nice harness to wear, and it worked wonders. Still, in general, I advise against harnessing your pup. As we began to train him and as he started to get stronger, it became clear that we needed a prong collar to help direct his behavior. Theo was able to throw his entire body behind his launches with a harness on, so we wanted to limit his power to what he could do with his neck muscles. Some people are highly averse to the prong collar, and I understand that. I just know that it works for us, and it works for Theo, allowing us to keep him safe. The Martingale collar is also an option, as well. This type of collar prevents a puppy from backing out of its collar and getting loose. This type of collar is a popular option for many owners.

Age-Appropriate Toys and Bones

If it has a squeaker, Theo will find it. Theo will extract the squeaker and play with just that tiny, easily choked upon part of the toy. For that reason, I recommend staying away from squeaky toys with your Anatolian. Your ASD is likely going to love to chew things. We prefer durable toys that last a decent amount of time but have given in to the fact that our dog's one objective is to destroy the toy beyond all recognition and then play with the remnants. Theo loves playing with rope, although he doesn't really go for tug-of-war. Kong makes some fantastic toys that are extremely durable, and Theo enjoys the ones made of durable plastic-like wheels and the large classic Kong toys. Anatolians aren't going to be your typical "go fetch" dog either, but we do use a lacrosse ball, as it is durable, and a big dog will be able to carry it in its mouth. While Theo enjoys having something good to chew on, he's not huge into playing with toys. So while we have them, Theo really has no interest. Give him a good bone, and he's more than content.

It is always important to monitor your puppy and adult dogs with bones as they can become fragmented, and your dog may choke on them. I recommend finding something that you can tolerate the smell of, and your ASD loves. Theo loves his goat horns. They do tend to smell a little bit at first, but we have gotten very used to them. We love how Theo is obsessed with them and how great they are for his dental health.

A Great Brush

This dog will shed. You are going to want to brush him multiple times a week, and you need to find a brush that is going to let you get at that undercoat and strip away all the dead hair that will find its way into your laundry, food, and furniture. Laura and I love to joke about how we find a "Theo hair" everywhere we go. You do not want to find "Theo hair." Trust me. We use a de-matting brush for Theo's fur, and it works wonders. You're not dealing with the

FUN FACT
Anatolian Shepherds on the Silver Screen

An Anatolian Shepherd was one of the stars of the 2001 action-comedy *Cats & Dogs*. The film follows warring factions of cats and dogs, who are secretly tech-savvy covert operatives with the ability to speak. Butch, a high-ranking member of the dogs' team, is played by an Anatolian Shepherd and voiced by Alec Baldwin.

same type of shedding as a Husky, but your ASD will still need a good brushing every few days. A professional-grade blow dryer is a great product to buy for their biannual coat shed, too. Also, invest in a great vacuum—you'll thank me later.

Food and Water-Related Supplies

Although ASDs are on the bigger side, you really do not need to purchase an elevated food and water stand as you might see for other large dogs. We have found it helpful to have a dedicated spot to put Theo's food. He no longer eats kibble (I'll explain later), but having a storage bin to pour kibble into that is airtight will ensure freshness and can also be a bit handier than just having the bag clipped in a pantry. A travel water dish is great for trips to the dog park while you're still able to go.

Grooming Supplies

A good set of nail clippers and Dremel will be your best friend when it comes to keeping your pup's nails in check. It is always important to get them comfortable with having their nails clipped and groomed as early as possible. But be sure not to force it upon them to the point that they turn and go the other way just by looking at the clippers. Theo is fine when we use the

Photo Courtesy
of Heidi Krol
Stonecoat Farm Anatolians

Dremel but will not allow his nails to be clipped under any circumstance. There was no traumatic experience for him with having his nails clipped since we brought him home, but for whatever reason, whether it be discomfort or fear, he does not let us do it. He is never aggressive, never snaps or snarls, but just immediately runs away like a child in trouble. It's not the worst thing in the world if you have a groomer do this for you, either.

You will also want preventative flea and tick treatments as well as heartworm treatments, especially if your dog will be outdoors/working.

Tearless shampoo and a microfiber cloth for baths will be instrumental to keeping your puppy clean.

Bedding and Crate Supplies

We enjoy having a nice, comfortable bed to sleep on. Surprise! Your dog is no different. It is always nice to have a decent bed for the dog to rest on, too. Your Anatolian is going to grow exponentially, so understand that getting a bed that may seem a little too big is perfectly fine! Dogs do prefer a denlike feel for their crate, as I mentioned before, so you may end up with two to three crates during your dog's lifetime—if you choose to crate train, of course. A good underlayment for the crate will prevent slipping and movement of the crate and preserve your flooring, too. You don't need to have a bed for inside of the crate and outside of the crate either, but that's a personal preference. A simple blanket or two will more than do the trick for laying down in the crate for your puppy (they'll probably chew them up, anyway).

Words of Wisdom

You're almost there! Giving yourself a great start is key to starting off your life with your new dog on the right foot. By considering what your needs are and what your dog's needs are, you are creating the essential framework for a happy and healthy relationship and environment for you both to thrive. Will you forget to buy something and quickly realize you need it? Absolutely! Will something suit your needs and your specific dog that I have not mentioned? I wouldn't bet against it. But by treating the above information as a sort of checklist, you will have more than enough ready for your pup's first days, weeks, and months together.

CHAPTER 5

Bringing Home Your Anatolian Shepherd

> "
>
> *They are extremely smart and independent. Expect a hard headed dog who will want to please you! Make sure you don't have lever door handles as they can open levers with their head and paws!*
>
> **PHILLIP SIMMONDS**
> *Simmonds Ranch*
>
> "

Depending on your exact circumstances, the ride home can take a few different forms. Something to keep in mind prior to picking your dog up is what your schedule looks like over the next week or so. Make sure you have free time to devote to getting your pup acclimated and comfortable. If you're going to have to leave the dog alone or with someone else during these crucial first days, do your best to find a better time or make arrangements so you can be there personally.

The Ride Home

I do not recommend picking up your ASD on your own. It will be useful to have someone keep their eyes on the road while you keep your eyes on the dog. It should be taken as the general rule to get your ASD as used to riding as far back in your vehicle as possible. The Anatolian Shepherd is keen on pegging itself at the top of any hierarchy, and the closer your dog is to being able to mimic your position, the more that he will come to believe that he is the same as you. For that reason, it is best to introduce your puppy or otherwise new dog to the vehicle in the back seat or furthermost trunk compartment. The passenger, who should be seated in the backseat and not the front passenger seat, can sit next to the puppy's crate while you keep your eyes on the road. Conversely, you can have someone else drive while you do these things.

Consider having the dog's crate in the back of your vehicle (if it fits) or have a harness that clicks into the seatbelt. Whatever you choose, you need to ensure that there is not enough slack to allow the dog to get somewhere it shouldn't or interfere with driving, and you must not let the dog be loose in the car. DO NOT put the dog on your lap when you're driving. A puppy who has no clue what your intentions are or where it is going can easily interfere with driving. Mix that with the 30-40-pound dog you're going to encounter at roughly 8-12 weeks (if you're picking up a puppy), and you'll immediately understand the danger. Furthermore, the front seat should always be off-limits for your dog. If there is an accident, the airbag will likely kill it immediately or cause terrible injuries.

WHAT TO BRING

Bring something with you like a blanket not only to comfort the dog but to protect your vehicle in case there are any sorts of accidents. To that point, bring some pet deodorizer/neutralizer. You'll want to bring a leash and collar

Photo Courtesy
of Bonnie Forrester

According to the AKC, the Anatolian Shepherd was the 90th most popular breed in America in 2020. This number is up from 94th most popular in 2019. The AKC determines popularity rankings based on the number of dogs registered from each breed.

as well as some treats. It may take some coaxing to get the pup into your vehicle at first, so those treats will come in handy. I would refrain from feeding him or giving him too much water before getting home as you run the risk of the dog having an accident or getting sick in the vehicle.

If you are picking the puppy up from a breeder, this will likely be his first time in a vehicle, so you are going to want to monitor how he handles the experience. Throwing a significant amount of food into the mix is just asking for trouble. If you are adopting, the dog will have likely been transported in a vehicle at some point, so you can ask the agency about any known aversions to riding in the car that you should know about. If you're in doubt about if the dog is hungry or thirsty, ask the people you are picking him up from. They can tell you what they recommend and how long ago the dog had something to drink or eat.

WALKS AND POTTY BREAKS ON THE WAY HOME

I recommend walking your pup prior to putting him in the car to tire him out a little bit so he'll mostly sleep on the way home. Ideally, he'll also go to the bathroom so that there will be no accidents once in the car. If you suspect that your pup needs to go to the bathroom or if it is a particularly long ride home, feel free to stop to walk him. However, DO NOT stop at a rest stop where there will be or have been many other dogs. This is particularly important if your pup has not been vaccinated yet, as he could be exposed to many diseases and germs. Once you arrive home, be sure to walk your pup again before bringing him into your house.

The First Night

The first night is going to be crucial. This is not a time to introduce the dog to any livestock, and I would even caution against allowing your other animals, if you have any, to see the puppy just yet. It is best to let the dog gain some sort of comfort with his new surroundings, whether predominantly indoor or outdoor, before making any critical introductions. This is the stage where having your plan mapped out will serve you. Having a hangout

Photo Courtesy of Cristina Padron

area, a crate/sleep area, and barriers up already will ensure that you have a systemic way to help acclimate your puppy to his new home. Make sure that his bed is where you want it and that the boundaries are clearly defined for where the dog can and cannot go. This will help establish you as the "pack leader" early on and make your life easier.

If you are anything like me, you're going to want to make sure your puppy doesn't have any accidents in your house if you can help it. I recommend bringing your Anatolian outside once every ninety minutes or so for that first night or even the first few nights. It may be a little excessive, but I wanted to make sure Theo was comfortable and that he would not have the added anxiety of having to pee or poop while sleeping in his crate at night.

Photo Courtesy
of Mason Taylor DeRosa

That brings me to another point: you need patience. Your dog will likely whine at night, especially if you are crate training. Remember that he is looking for a response from you! You need to be tough and not give him the response he wants, or you are simply reinforcing the behavior. If you want your dog in a specific area of the house (if not in a crate), resist the temptation to put him in your bed with you. I have found that Anatolians are not the biggest cuddlers anyway, but their sheer size upon reaching maturity should be enough to dissuade you from creating that habit.

Choosing A Veterinarian and the First Vet Visit

Hand in hand with the preparation for your pup's first night with you is having the right vet already chosen and the first vet visit planned for as soon as possible after you bring your dog home. Choosing the right vet is like trying on a pair of shoes: when you know, you know. It is important to get a full sense of what veterinarians are in your area and what their philosophies are. A driving factor behind your choice should be the location and hours of availability in case of emergency. But also, it's particularly important to know whether your vet works well with large or small breed dogs. Some vets believe in a more holistic approach to nutrition and medicine, while others may not. Both approaches have pros and cons. It's important to note what is contained in your breeder's contract to ensure you are not going against any stipulations.

You can get a particularly good sense of a vet from the reception team. Call around and see how you are treated on the phone! Ask questions not just about bringing in your puppy for a first visit but what subsequent encounters might look like. It's always great to know that your pup will be treated as a priority.

Your first vet visit will involve the vet taking your dog's weight. The vet will ask how your puppy has been eating and drinking, if his stools look regular, and if he is adjusting well to your house/property.

Your puppy will get his first round of shots, which can vary depending on your geographical region, but the typical ones include flea and tick, heartworm, rabies, and a distemper shot. The vet will ask about whether you will be getting your animal spayed or neutered and will recommend the best time to do so. Some vets will say to wait until the dog is at least a year, while others say it should be done as soon as possible.

Make the vet experience as comfortable and easy as possible for your puppy. It all starts with picking the right vet that not only makes sense geographically but has beliefs that align with your own. You wouldn't want to go see a doctor that you fundamentally disagree with, right?

CHAPTER 6
Housetraining

Nothing is better than having a well-trained dog who knows that the restroom is outside. Unfortunately, it is going to take a bit of time and practice for both of you to get to that point. Luckily, there are several things that can be done to housetrain your Anatolian and get him used to holding it until he can make it outdoors.

Photo Courtesy of Krista Young

Set Expectations and Be Realistic

One of the biggest parts of housetraining a puppy is having clear and realistic expectations for your new family member. Sure, it's easy to get frustrated when he goes to the bathroom on your carpet or on your beloved area rug, but that frustration needs to be minimized for your own health and for your pup's mental health. Dogs can easily sense your frustration, and nothing is worse than if they believe that they are the source of your anger. It's vital to the success of both of you that, as the "boss," you keep your composure and remain your pup's biggest fan when he successfully goes to the bathroom outdoors and in the desired location.

You can't expect that there won't be accidents along the way. You're going to end up sorely disappointed and unprepared for when the inevitable occurs. So, keeping that idea of realistic expectations in mind, what can you do to ensure your puppy's success?

Options for Potty Training

I can only speak personally to the method that Laura and I used to train Theo. Theo came to us at about 12 weeks old with his main vaccinations and everything he needed to safely be outdoors without facing any health concerns. This is not the case for every puppy! So, while I will speak at length in this chapter about how to get your puppy to understand that going to the bathroom outdoors is where he should go, it's not the only option available to you, especially if your dog does not have the required shots to be safe outdoors.

There are such things as doggy potties that can be utilized by puppies until they are able to go outdoors safely. However, the Anatolian is not a suitable candidate to use one of these. Plus, training your dog to go to the bathroom indoors isn't something that any Anatolian owner would advise. The Anatolian is a large dog, and the breed is naturally independent. Get them outdoors!

FUN FACT
Anatolian Shepherds on the Silver Screen

Kate and Leopold is a 2001 romantic comedy about a time-traveling duke in New York City. The film features Hugh Jackman and Meg Ryan, who share the screen with an Anatolian Shepherd named "Bart" in the film. Bart was played by a two-and-a-half-year-old pup named Noah.

REARRANGE AND MODIFY A FEW THINGS

Let's say you've got that area rug you just love so much and was so expensive (but gotten on sale, of course). Roll it up. Unless you want something to be upset about, limit your pup's ability to upset you and your family with accidents. Maybe your dining room or family room looks a little strange to you with no rug, but it's only going to be temporary. Trust me; if my wife can sacrifice her love for feng shui long enough to ensure that Theo is housetrained and unable to ruin anything important, you can do so as well! While you're at it, cover up those couches and recliners. I've never seen my dog or any dog pee on top of a couch, but hey, it's happened to someone, somewhere. Don't let it happen to you.

Keep the pup limited to as few areas as possible to limit the potential for accidents in your bedroom, bathroom, basement, or kitchen. Sometimes these areas don't have doors and are hard to wall off, but figure out a good way that works for you. Baby gates and x-pens are reliable options for many owners who are looking to keep their dogs out of trouble and protect their houses from incidents.

Laura and I made the mistake of allowing Theo to roam around from the living room to the kitchen to our bedroom when we were house training. We knew that if he was in the bedroom for too long, we'd likely have a nice present waiting on the floor for us. These are not the presents you want. Trust me. Keep your pup within sight, and if you can, keep him in one room of the house for this crucial period. You'll thank yourself and me down the road when you're saving on carpet cleanings.

CLEANING UP ACCIDENTS

Accidents will be a part of your reality as a new dog owner, and that's okay. You're going to want to have an enzymatic cleaner on hand throughout your pup's entire life. I recommend this type of cleaner because they're second to none at breaking down stains and actually removing odors as opposed to just covering them up. This will help prevent your dog from continuing to soil the same spots and deter the behavior altogether. You're going to find that there are plenty of cleaners that contain enzymes, so be on the lookout for ones that also work as multipurpose cleaners. Having this type in stock will also allow you to easily clean up mud or stains your pup might track into the house. A good product to consider picking up that Laura and I use is the Rocco and Roxie Professional Strength Stain & Odor Eliminator. You're welcome.

The First Few Weeks

I'm not going to lie to you: it's going to be challenging. It's certainly an adjustment if you've never had a dog or never had to potty train an animal before. You're going to need to allot plenty of time to go outside and walk your pup or simply be out there to observe that he's using the bathroom. (I don't recommend leaving your puppy unsupervised at all at this stage, anyway). This means rain, sleet, snow, and everything in between. You must be committed to this for it to be effective!

HOW TO KNOW WHEN HE HAS TO GO

The million-dollar question! Puppies are hard to time, and Anatolians are notoriously known for getting a bit distracted when they're taken out to use the bathroom. Remaining diligent and keeping your puppy focused on going pee or poop is going to take time and effort, but it is a vital step.

There are some telltale signs that can be observed that will send you the message that your dog has got to go. When Theo was a puppy, if he began sniffing around on the floor, it was a sign that he was searching for a place to go to the bathroom. If your dog begins circling or pacing around the room, this should also be taken as a sign that he needs to go. Theo did these two things very often, and it should be easy to detect when your puppy's behavior just seems a little "off." More obvious signs are when he starts to whine, bark, or scratch at the door that leads to the doggy potty or outside. When you get to the stage that your puppy begins doing this, it's a great sign because it means he's associating going to the bathroom with the desired location.

FREQUENCY

The general rule of "less is more" does not apply to outdoor trips to use the bathroom. Puppies have a difficult time controlling their bladders, have smaller bladders, and don't understand yet that they can't just go wherever they want. When we got Theo, we were taking him out at least once every two hours. At least that frequently, and oftentimes more often. At first, your pup isn't going to connect being outside with going to the bathroom. In his mind, it's going to be a place that he just happens to be going to the bathroom, but it's not the reason that he's out there. By creating an excess of opportunity for him to go to the bathroom outside, he'll begin to put it together that this is where he's supposed to go.

Rewarding Correct Behavior

I'm going to state this from the very beginning: be enthusiastic and bring treats! Dogs need to understand that they've done the correct thing. So, from the very earliest time possible, be so enthusiastic about letting him know how proud you are of him for going to the bathroom in the right place that it seems excessive. Praise him like this when he goes on the pads in the house, too.

Dogs are extrinsically motivated by treats and food. Use this to your advantage. Couple your enthusiastic praise with a treat to let your pup know how happy you are that he did what he was supposed to do! He'll eventually put together that when he eliminates outdoors or in the correct area, he is rewarded for it. This will help speed up the training process and create a stronger bond between the two of you.

HOW NOT TO REACT

It is wise to reconsider punishing your puppy for accidents in the house or in their crate. The reality is that your dog is not going to know why you are upset with him by you yelling or acting upset with them. Whether they had the accident five minutes or five hours ago, they're not going to make that connection. A mistake that first-time dog owners make is thinking that rubbing their pup's nose in their feces or urine will train them to not have accidents any longer. Never, ever, ever, do this. Your dog will learn that you are to be feared and can develop deep psychological problems and simply hide when they need to use the bathroom. Again, do not, under any circumstance, rub your dog's nose in their feces or urine.

If you react in a hostile manner, you are also potentially weakening the bond you are trying to foster with your pup. If your dog becomes fearful of you or loses trust, he will likely listen to you even less. Another rule of thumb is to avoid raising your voice at all in this situation. Dogs that are yelled at frequently can begin submissively urinating to demonstrate that they are not a threat to you. This is obviously not something you want to occur.

The general rule of thumb here is to be patient. Do not freak out at your dog when he has an accident in the house. It's not natural for them to hold their bladder, and it's going to be something that takes time. Your patience will be rewarded.

Crate Training for Housetraining Use

Crate training is one of those topics that some people are in favor of, and others are against. I will tell you that my experience with crate training has only been positive. It gave my wife and me peace of mind while we were away and could not bring Theo with us as a puppy. But more importantly, the crate was a source of comfort for Theo as a pup so that when we were gone, we knew that he would feel safe and secure. This brings me to my first point.

USE THE CRATE FOR GOOD

Many people who begin crate training do so for all the right reasons. They want their dog to be crated when they're not home and when they are asleep at night to make sure that the dog stays out of trouble and out of danger. Logic would then tell us that the crate should be a place that the dog is comfortable and goes to relax or hang out during the day. But the crate can often turn into something else altogether.

It's all too easy to begin using the crate to punish your dog. And if the dog begins to associate the crate with punishment, he will freak out in the crate when you leave him home alone or at nighttime when you'd like to get some sleep. Here are the steps that you should take if you wish to crate train your dog effectively.

CHOOSE THE RIGHT CRATE

Remember that less is more with your Anatolian's crate. You'll likely end up with multiple crates to take your dog from puppy to adult but always err on the side of smaller to provide the "den" that dogs enjoy. For a full break-down of how to choose the right crate, refer back to chapter four.

GET YOUR DOG IN THE RIGHT FRAME OF MIND

I've mentioned this before, but it cannot be overstated. You must ensure that your dog associates the crate with relaxation. If you put him in the crate when he's stressed, he'll associate the crate with stress. If you put him in there while he's playing, he'll want to get out to keep playing. Put him in the crate while he's calm and relaxed, so that will be what he associates the crate with.

FIGURE OUT YOUR DOG'S COMFORT LEVEL

Decide if you want to provide a bed for the crate or whether you'll simply put some blankets or towels down. When Theo was a puppy, and we were going through the crate training process, we made the mistake of putting a nice, plush, expensive bed in his crate. Well, let's just say that one day we came home, and it looked like someone put the bed through an industrial shredder. Your best bet is going to be to either opt for no bed or something very inexpensive, at least to start.

REWARD GOOD BEHAVIOR

Just as you praise and reward for good potty training, you need to do the same thing with the crate. Create that positive association between being in the crate and your dog. Give him a KONG with frozen peanut butter (Theo loves those) and let him enjoy that while he's in the crate. This way, your dog will associate crate time with something enjoyable.

BE MINDFUL OF TIME

Make sure your dog is not in the crate for too long, especially as a puppy. Dogs will only go to the bathroom in their crate as an absolute last resort, even as puppies. If your dog is soiling the crate, it likely means he's been left in the crate too long, or it could be an indication of a health problem such as a UTI.

MAKE A GAME OF IT

Again, the crate cannot have a negative association for your dog if it's going to be successful. Work on getting your dog in and out of the crate during playtime. Throw the ball in the crate or put some treats in the crate for him to find. Whatever it takes and whatever works best to create that positive mindset!

NO COLLARS OR CLOTHES

Be sure to remove anything from your dog's body that can get snagged on the crate. The last thing anyone wants is for a totally avoidable tragedy to occur.

LET SUCCESS BE YOUR GOAL

If you want your dog to succeed, do everything you can to make sure that will occur! Start by leaving for small spurts of time. With Theo, Laura and I would put him in the crate, grab our keys, and walk out the door. We weren't actually going anywhere, but we wanted Theo to think that we were. After a minute or two, we'd walk back in so he could see that we would be coming back when we left. This little step did wonders to build his confidence in the crate and allowed us to start going places for short time frames. Once he stopped whining when we initially left, we would go to the gas station or to the deli and quickly come back.

We gradually increased the duration of our trips until Theo became totally comfortable being in his crate for a few hours at a time. We always made sure to give plenty of praise and treats to our good boy when we got back and let him out. Think about getting a pet camera as well so you can see how he is acting when you're out. If you see and hear that he's whining while you're away, adjust your plan.

HAVE PATIENCE

It's going to take some time to crate train. It's going to test your will and your discipline, too. Laura and I struggled when crate training Theo because we felt so bad when he'd whine and whimper. But we knew we had to be tough if we wanted to get through it and for all our work and Theo's to be worth it. Expect full crate training to take at least six months to accomplish and very possibly longer, although it can be a much quicker process for some dogs. Make sure you stay consistent even when it becomes difficult, and keep the end goal in mind.

Leaving Your Dog Home Alone

If your dog is not properly house trained, keeping your dog crated whenever you leave the house is my solution. It is what is best for him and for you. You don't want to have any lingering thoughts in your head about what your dog is up to while you're away. If you have other animals in the house, this is especially important because you simply don't know what can happen when they're unsupervised.

Keep in mind the overall size of the Anatolian, as well. When he reaches maturity, he can easily knock his nose on the gas burner switches on your stove and jostle it just enough to have some gas come out and start a fire. Sound horrific? It is, so spare yourself the mental anguish and keep your pup in the crate. That said, never leave him in there for over eight hours. Like I mentioned above, give him something like a KONG with peanut butter or something that can be safely consumed (refrain from bones) unsupervised. Remember that you need to gradually ease into leaving your dog alone.

If you're not crate training your dog, the same principles apply that I mentioned above. Keep your dog somewhere he can be comfortable and where he will not get himself into any danger. Playpens and baby gates will likely not be a solution here as Anatolians will easily hop over either if left unsupervised—especially if something catches their eye that they'd like to investigate. Many owners suggest using x-pens between 42 and 48 inches to keep your Anatolian contained.

Whatever your method is, whether in a room with some blankets and toys or a crate, I really suggest keeping your dog from roaming around freely unsupervised. I'll be completely honest with you: Laura and I have left Theo home alone with our two cats unsupervised. Was there a disaster when we got back? No. But were we stressed the entire time thinking there would be? Absolutely. That's why we minimize Theo's ability to do himself or anything else harm. We're never gone too long to the point we feel that we are neglectful, and Theo is comfortable enough in his crate where he just enjoys a treat and usually catches up on some sleep. It's really your best bet with an Anatolian.

CHAPTER 7

Socializing with People and Animals

> *Socializing with other dogs is best done off your property because Anatolians are protective of their territories. Take your puppy to obedience class to meet other dogs under controlled circumstances. Visiting dog shows is another good option because the dogs there are well-trained. Avoid dog parks and other off-leash areas. Anatolians should not be let loose with unfamiliar dogs as they can respond aggressively when challenged and may injure other dogs.*
>
> NANCY BURNS
> *Marble Peaks Ranch*

It's no secret that a well-socialized dog is very desirable. Just about everyone loves to have a dog that is easily approachable, good with kids, great with other dogs, and with all other animals. I will be the first to tell you that the Anatolian is generally going to appear to be very calm and great with other animals and dogs and people when young. However, as the dog matures, his naturally territorial instincts are going to become very visible and will begin to present challenges that you will need to overcome through discipline, love, and a healthy dose of consistent training.

I've mentioned already that when Theo began to show his Anatolian instincts as he got older, it was such a shock that Laura and I really did not know what to do. This shift in behavior was what got us to look deep into the breed to find out all we could so we could know if this was a phase or if this was what he was going to be like. Luckily, there are ways to socialize an Anatolian and make it comfortable in various settings and around other animals. While you're not going to undo his naturally protective and dominant personality, you can help him adjust to situations and settings where he will need to behave in certain ways.

The Importance of Good Socialization

Socialization is one of those buzzwords in the dog universe. Many people throw it around, but very few explain what it entails when done correctly. It's certainly not as easy as just bringing your Anatolian to a dog park and telling him to have fun and run around; in fact, you're not going to bring your Anatolian to dog parks! It's not as difficult as a complex algebra problem, either. The key to having the best socialization possible for your dog really comes down to understanding the when, the why, and the how.

WHEN SHOULD I BEGIN SOCIALIZING?

Socialization should ideally begin with the breeder to help positively shape your dog's personality and continue as soon as you bring him home. When you purchase a dog, it's tough to determine how much socialization he has already had since his background can be a big question mark but begin the process as soon as the dog is officially yours.

Photo Courtesy
of Cristina Padron

Photo Courtesy of Ashley Clement

A professional breeder should have begun to socialize the puppy within the first weeks of his life through gentle and loving handling and by introducing new sights, smells, situations, people, and other dogs and animals to them in a safe environment. Dogs are just like people in that the experiences they have when they are young are formative; they're being shaped into the type of dog they will be in the future. A calm, confident, and gentle dog is shaped from birth by exposing him to situations that will reinforce and encourage those characteristics.

WHY SHOULD I SOCIALIZE MY ANATOLIAN?

The benefits of proper socialization are numerous, and I would say that socializing a dog is as necessary as socializing a child. Just like humans, dogs are social creatures, and part of their emotional growth is vitally connected to the socialization process. Believe it or not, the number one cause of death in dogs under three years of age is behavioral issues, not any type of disease. By socializing your pup, you may just be saving his life. If you're seeking a well-mannered companion who is not fearful of children, adults, or car rides, begin the process as soon as you can and as soon as your veterinarian gives the okay. Take your Anatolian to public places, let him be around other people, and ensure that he is always in a safe situation that you are in control of.

How to Socialize the Anatolian Shepherd

What makes the Anatolian such an interesting and awesome dog is its overall versatility! While many of you reading this will be purchasing or adopting an Anatolian as a companion, many will also be looking to purchase a working animal that will be as comfortable around livestock as it will be around children and other smaller animals/pets. In this section, I'll give you all the basics for how to socialize your pup, which will be beneficial in getting him comfortable with other pets and children, and also give you some ideas of how to introduce him to your livestock.

ALWAYS BE POSITIVE

Dogs can read our emotions so well. I think they know our emotions better than we do, even! Make sure that every situation you introduce your puppy to is a positive one! Always provide lots of praise and lots of treats in these situations so that your dog associates these new experiences with things he enjoys. Make sure that you yourself are relaxed since any fear and anxiety we have is easily transferred down a leash to a puppy.

THE WORLD IS A BUFFET

No, I don't mean that your puppy should be encouraged to eat everything (although he might enjoy that). Instead, try to have your dog meet and experience as many things as possible. Introduce him to people with beards, disabilities, people of different ethnicities, and people who are wearing wide varieties of clothing. Take him to visit urban areas, rural areas, and everything in between. I can think of countless things to introduce your dog to. Never miss an opportunity to show your dog that it's a safe situation or a safe person to be around.

When we were socializing Theo, we found that simply bringing him places with us (dog permitting) was a great way to expose him to all sorts of situations. Whether we brought him to a department store where he could walk on an unfamiliar floor, an outdoor restaurant, a public walking bridge, or to a brewery, we knew that he would encounter people, smells, and situations that would benefit his development.

BUT DON'T "EAT" TOO QUICK

You want to be careful not to overstimulate your pup. Slowly introduce him to new things and settings and try not to feel the urge to squeeze multiple happenings into one day or put your puppy into a situation that is too busy or overstimulating. Do not bring your puppy to new places before he's been vaccinated or is comfortable around your family members and some friends.

When introducing your puppy to new people, start with your own family members. Once your puppy is acclimated to being around your children and then perhaps some extended family members, move on to introducing a friend along with a family member. Once your dog is comfortable in that situation, then, perhaps, think about moving on to allowing strangers to be introduced to your pup.

Socializing with Other Dogs

> "
>
> *They are a very independent dog and can be quite dominant. Be sure to do all the research you can and make sure you can handle a dog with a mind of their own. They definitely need to be introduced and socialized with other people and dogs as they tend to become territorial and possessive of their owners.*
>
> **PHILLIP SIMMONDS**
> *Simmonds Ranch*
>
> "

As a dog owner, you're going to run into plenty of other dog owners. Your pup and theirs are going to be naturally curious about each other, but you've got to keep a few things in mind before just letting them sniff each other.

Look at each dog's physical cues and demeanor. Any signs of agitation from either dog are an immediate reason to separate them. Raised hackles, baring of teeth, or solid stares are the usual cues, along with growling and lip curling. As the one in control, avoid tension on the leash as your tension travels down the leash to your dog. If they sense that you are uneasy, it will likely make them uneasy. If you're calm, they're more likely to remain calm. Don't allow your dog or theirs to rush towards the other without closely watching their behavior. Things could go well in this scenario, but play could escalate into a fight if you're not careful.

If both dogs appear calm, a good place to start is by having the dogs walk across from each other at a safe distance and see if they remain calm. Allow the dogs to smell the area that the other has been to get acclimated with their scent. If all is going well at this point, consider allowing the dogs to move closer to one another. Be wary of allowing the dogs to go nose to nose while meeting. This can put some dogs in a very vulnerable position, making them uneasy. If you see the dogs in this position, consider separating the dogs.

If things appear to be going well to this point and you can find an enclosed area to let the dogs interact with minimal hovering from their handlers, give that a go.

Like other learning situations, give your pup verbal guidance. If they're doing well, praise them. If they need correction, use verbal cues. This is really the only interference your pup will find useful from you.

It is worth a reminder that Anatolians are not really the type of dog you go around introducing to other dogs on a whim. Careful consideration needs to be made about what you are trying to accomplish by introducing your dog to others.

YOU ARE YOUR DOG'S PROTECTOR

You absolutely have no obligation to let someone else's dog near yours. I actually don't recommend having your Anatolian around other dogs until your pup is trained and until you have met the other dog yourself. You would not believe the amount of poorly trained (or not trained at all) dogs that are out there. Your Anatolian might be big as a puppy, but he is still a puppy. One bad interaction with another dog as a puppy can do a lifetime of damage for your Anatolian. Be extremely careful when walking your pup and seeing another dog. Don't be afraid to say no to someone if they ask if they can pet your dog or allow their dog to get near yours. They might think you're rude, but any good dog owner understands a no to this request.

FUN FACT
Anatolian Shepherds in Yellowstone

Two Anatolian Shepherd puppies named Karabaş and Akbaş were sent to Yellowstone National Park in 2017 as part of an effort to protect wildlife. These "fluffy" rangers work as a barrier between wild predators and domesticated livestock and human visitors. Anatolian Shepherds are deployed in similar settings across the globe and serve as a nonlethal defense against predators that allows livestock and wildlife to coexist in these spaces.

PUPPY TRAINING CLASSES

Puppy training classes are a great way to get your puppy used to being around other dogs and provide him with mental stimulation. Once your dog can be safely in public and around other animals without safety concerns, consider enrolling him in a class. I will discuss these classes at greater length in chapter nine, but a proper puppy trainer will be able to run the class comfortably and confidently with no compromise to the safety of any dog or person involved. You can find information about where to sign your Anatolian up through the AKC or through your local pet stores/training facilities.

THE DOG PARK

When Theo was a puppy, Laura and I would consistently bring him to the dog park nearby three or four times a week to let him socialize and get a good deal of exercise. He loved it, and we loved it. We really enjoyed everyone telling us how handsome our big man was even as we dealt with that "big dog stigma" I mentioned in chapter one.

As Theo got a little older, he started to become extremely territorial about the park. He was never aggressive with the other dogs, but he'd growl or bark a bit more often than we'd ever known him to, which was a bit of a concern but nothing to dissuade us from bringing him. But as he

*Photo Courtesy
of Heidi Krol
Stonecoat Farm Anatolians*

continued to get older, he kept barking and growling, and although we knew he was gentle and great with other dogs, he was a big puppy and certainly intimidating.

We started to gradually bring him less and less as it became clearly stressful for Theo and for us, and honestly, a bit embarrassing. When we began researching more about the Anatolian Shepherd, we realized that Theo was, by nature, a very territorial species, and his behavior immediately made sense to us.

It was unfortunate that we couldn't bring him to the dog park to play with the dogs like he always had, but we knew it was best for him. We no longer bring him to any dog parks, as his territorial instinct began to fully form at around six months, and he decided the park belonged to him, and he didn't particularly enjoy other dogs coming and going as they pleased.

As a new Anatolian Shepherd owner, it is imperative that you do not make the same mistakes that I made. Experienced Anatolian owners will tell you to simply refrain from bringing this dog to any type of dog park. It is in the best interest of your dog, and the risks highly outweigh the rewards.

Introducing Your Dog to Unfamiliar Children

As a puppy, your Anatolian Shepherd is probably going to be quite docile, and children are going to want to come right up to him and pet the big boy. You know your dog best. I mentioned before that you are your dog's protector when it comes to saying no to having other dogs approach him; the same goes for children. All it takes is one bad moment or one misplaced hand from a child for you and your dog to get into a world of trouble. Don't be scared to say no when a parent or a child asks to pet your dog. They'll live. Be on the lookout for signs of stress exhibited by your dog. Yawning, lip-licking, and panting are all signs that your dog is feeling distressed. If you notice these signs, it is best to avoid allowing the child to approach your dog.

If you know your dog's temperament and are confident that they're not showing any signs of distress, you can allow the child to approach your pup. You need to communicate clearly that they should pet your dog under the chin or on the side of the head as opposed to on top and to pet slowly. Let them know to avoid the eyes and the ears, as those are sensitive, too. Most kids will know not to pull ears or tails, but you should make sure that that's clear because kids can be too quick to correct on the fly. Through all of this, make sure your overall tone is gentle and calm with the child. Kids are naturally curious and want to do the right thing, and they will with your guidance.

CHAPTER 8
Physical and Mental Exercise

Part of owning any dog is acknowledging the responsibility you now must ensure that your pup is not only fed and loved but stimulated physically and mentally. I really stress the importance of the mental side of this because this is the area that is most likely to get overlooked. Physical and mental training are equally important.

When Laura and I brought Theo home, we were unsure of how to best go about getting him the physical exercise he needed. Truthfully, we hardly even thought about the mental aspect because we figured, hey, he's a big dog and is going to need as much exercise as possible. Remember, we didn't know he was an Anatolian Shepherd when we adopted him, let alone know how to take care of one. So, we took Theo on countless walks (he was fully

vaccinated and "ready to go" when we adopted) and got a membership to a local dog park to help with socialization and keep him active. He looked so goofy, running around on his massive paws chasing the older and mostly smaller dogs.

Something we noticed right away was that Theo either got physically tired very quickly (to be expected as a puppy) or simply grew tired of playing with the other dogs and would simply plop down with a ball between his paws and "happy pant" while looking at us or the other dogs playing. Laura and I weren't worried at all by this since we knew that puppies typically tire faster than full-grown dogs. As we discovered that Theo was an Anatolian Shepherd, we wanted to find out exactly how we should best approach mental and physical exercise for Theo.

FUN FACT
Lieutenant Robert Ballard

After a failed attempt to introduce Anatolian Shepherds in America by the US government during a 1930s top-secret "Sheepdog Project," a sailor in the US Navy separately brought a pair of these dogs home. Lieutenant Robert Ballard was stationed in Turkey in the 1960s and returned to America with two Anatolian Shepherds, from whom he bred his first litter in 1970. This litter is considered to be foundational to the breed in America.

Exercise Requirements

Anatolian Shepherds really don't need as much physical exercise as you may expect compared to other large breed dogs. They are moderately active, but they don't need to run miles a day to stay in shape. I'll cover their nutritional needs in a later chapter, but since this dog doesn't tend to overeat, they tend to have a more muscular frame and, in general, will not become overweight. While an Anatolian Shepherd is not a couch potato, they're probably at a "5" on an activity level scale out of 10.

GENERAL PUPPY EXERCISE

A good mix of physical and mental stimulation is essential to your pup's development. Remember, the Anatolian is extremely smart and has been bred to be an independent thinker. You need to embrace this quality from the start and feed your dog's desire to think and act. Whether it's hiding treats for him to find or playing with a ball outside, keep your puppy's activity level high and try to mix together the mental and physical play. Anatolians will benefit from play that has meaning to it, as they're not really huge fans of mindless fetch games or just running after a ball.

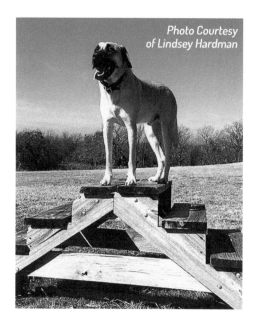

Photo Courtesy of Lindsey Hardman

We utilized the dog park quite extensively when Theo was only a few months old so he could socialize and run around to get rid of his energy. He wasn't big on running after the ball when we threw it, but he was very interested when other dogs went for it because his territorial instinct must have told him, "that's my ball, and I might not want it right now, but I definitely don't want them to have it." Overall, I'd say the more physical and mental exercise, the better. Anatolians will let you know when they've had enough or are too tired and won't grind themselves down trying to keep up. They're very much on their own time when it comes to the desire to partake in physical and mental games.

PHYSICAL & MENTAL STIMULATION FOR ADULTS

Now that Theo has officially (oh, where does the time go?) reached adulthood, Laura and I still seek ways to mentally stimulate him along with physical exercise. In our house, we constantly do training drills that require him to be disciplined and to use his brain. To receive his meal, he must go to his "place" (bed) and sit. He cannot eat his food until we have given him the word that it is okay. This is mentally taxing on a dog when you're first teaching him this! Think about his drive to simply see food and eat it. You're making him go against his primal instinct to simply gorge himself on some tasty food. But it's good for his mental health because it gets them thinking!

Laura and I look for all sorts of opportunities to keep Theo's mind active throughout the day by giving him tasks like finding a certain toy we've hidden in the house or finding treats we've hidden. We find this especially important since he's not a working dog, so we know that part of him is really missing that mental stimulation that his instincts call for.

We keep his physical activity a priority, too. Laura and I bring him on three or four 30-minute walks a day, and Theo also spends a couple of hours a week at a doggy daycare so that he can play with other dogs and also have a large space to run around on his own.

How to Keep Your Anatolian Physically Engaged

We took young Theo on several walks a day, ranging from 30-60 minutes. Nothing crazy and no crazy hiking trails, although we did do an occasional hike when he was a few months old. When we would take Theo to the dog park, we found about 30 minutes to an hour of playtime was enough to get him nice and tuckered. Anatolians are exceptionally good about letting you and other dogs know when they've had enough playtime and exercise.

Whether you simply plan to take your ASD on walks or take them to a dog park, I recommend that you try to combine the two at least one or two days a week to keep your young dog active and socializing. And remember what I stated above about giving the activity meaning. Anatolians will quickly lose interest in the activity if it is not challenging them in some way.

How to Keep Your Anatolian Mentally Engaged

As I mentioned before, mental stimulation is so important. Most of this mental stimulation will come in the form of training and repetition of commands. I will be covering these commands in detail in chapter nine but understand that the Anatolian was bred to work and to think independently. This dog craves the mental stimulation that working provides. Whether your pup is going to be a house or field dog will determine the types of mental stimulation it is exposed to on a regular basis, but keeping him stimulated early on as a puppy is particularly important. You want his mind to be sharp and for him to get used to listening to you at the same time. Mental exercise is also physically tiring for your ASD. Think about times you've taken a tough exam and have been physically exhausted when you were done. That's what it's like when your pup is using a lot of his brainpower during training and through vigorous mental repetition. Regular mental exercise is great for long-term brain health and goes hand in hand with physical health.

CHAPTER 9
Training Your Anatolian Shepherd

> "
>
> *The Anatolian Shepherd has been bred for thousands of generations to think and act independently in order to protect flocks against predators when no humans are present. This is a direct contrast to the majority of companion or sporting breeds that have been selected for following direct human guidance. An ASD evaluates your commands rather than following them with slavish loyalty. You must demonstrate to an ASD that there is a good reason for comply with your instructions. The new owner should be patient and consistent and seek mutual respect between human and dog. An Anatolian is a partner, not a servant.*
>
> **NANCY BURNS**
> *Marble Peaks Ranch*
>
> "

As I've mentioned throughout, training your Anatolian Shepherd is critical to having a happy and successful life together. Training isn't going to be a one-time thing that you simply start when he is a puppy and end when you think he's got the basic commands down. No, it's going to be a lifelong exercise if you are going to be successful.

When Laura and I got Theo, we wanted a housedog that would listen to us and be able to follow all the basic commands like sit, stay, etc. When we learned about his breed and learned just how headstrong an Anatolian could be, I can't lie; we panicked just a little bit. We were fully prepared to train a puppy the way you would think would be sufficient. Puppy training classes, maybe an intermediate class, and consistency with our at-home commands quickly became the bare minimum on our minds for how to train Theo the most effective way. Luckily, as we grew along with Theo, we were

able to find a reputable trainer who understood the nature of the Anatolian Shepherd and was able to train Laura and me at the same time.

Maybe the biggest piece of advice I can give at the start of this chapter is that you will also undergo training along with your pup. You need to have an open mind and be willing to work just as hard as your dog throughout the process if you want to be successful—you'll even need to outsmart your dog much of the time! Having a well-trained and good-mannered Anatolian is going to be an incredibly challenging but incredibly rewarding journey. It will test your patience and his patience, but your pup craves discipline, and your bond will only grow stronger throughout the process if the training is done properly. Luckily, the Anatolian is a very trainable dog, although they will always have an independent disposition. The key will be consistency, and I will continue to stress that throughout this book.

Puppy Training

Luckily for Laura and me, we live near quite a few commercial and locally-owned training centers. When we first got Theo, we had no intention of taking him through rigorous training programs with a private trainer, so we first investigated some generic puppy training classes. He was fully vaccinated, and we felt like it would be great for his socialization, along with teaching him some great commands and manners while around other dogs. So, Laura spearheaded the effort to find the proper training program for Theo and ultimately settled on the puppy training classes offered by our local PetSmart. Yeah, not the most unique or exciting training selection, but we knew a few people who had taken their dogs there, and the trainer that ran the program had an exceptionally good reputation, so we felt comfortable with the offering.

Looking back, it would be easy to say that Theo needed something more intense than the group sessions offered through PetSmart's puppy training course, but I honestly recommend group-based, positive reinforcement-oriented training as early as possible. It's not going to be enough, mind you, but it is a great warm-up for both you and your dog. If you think of these early puppy training classes as training for you and your dog and approach it with the mindset that you're there to learn as much as he is, you'll flourish in the course and in any subsequent courses that you may choose to take.

As for the class itself, a good puppy training class will typically provide a small-group setting with a credentialed trainer. Make sure that you know the trainer's credentials and certifications prior to paying any type of money. Whether it be a trainer that is part of the APDT or one that's passed the prestigious Karen Pryor training program, certification matters immensely! Meet the trainer, too, beforehand. After all, this person is going to be influencing the behavior of your pup, as well as your own!

Benefits of Proper Training

The benefits of having a properly trained dog are numerous. Most people have encountered a dog that is misbehaved and doesn't have any manners. Guess what? It's not the dog's fault! He's simply being a dog. If you are living in a suburb, it is mandatory that your Anatolian be very well trained as early as possible, as the later they are trained, the harder it is going to become. It's on the owners to ensure that their dog has the proper instruction and training to allow him to be well behaved. Since you're reading this, you are going to be in the minority when it comes to having a dog that is a model for good behavior, and you and your dog will enjoy the many fruits (and treats) that good training brings.

By having a well-trained dog, you will be able to bring him with you on adventures that you otherwise could not. Whether an afternoon outing to a winery, a hike, or to a family barbecue, not having to worry about your dog getting into trouble or being a handful is worth every penny and second of training. You are certainly going to still face challenges when taking your Anatolian anywhere, but training really does matter in this regard. Remember, Anatolians are big dogs, so every time they do something that others may perceive as "out of line," it's going to be amplified due to their size. Think of the peace of mind that you will have knowing that your dog will behave whenever you leave it alone and that it will listen to you in virtually any situation. I'm not going to lie to you; it's going to be a struggle to train your Anatolian to a level where he listens to you most of the time, but with this type of dog, "most of the time" can be considered a huge victory.

FUN FACT
Livestock Guarding Dog Program

It's well known that Anatolian Shepherds are excellent at protecting sheep, but did you know that they also protect cheetahs in parts of the world? Cheetahs are a protected species in Namibia, but these feline predators, with their ability to kill large numbers of sheep in a short period of time, can be devastating to sheep farmers, making them a prime target for illegal hunting. Since 1994, however, the Livestock Guarding Dog Program has been bringing dogs to Namibia to protect sheep, which in turn protects cheetahs, who are deathly afraid of these large dogs.

If your dog is working with livestock, you obviously can't expect an untrained pup to reliably accomplish any type of task without proper training. The efficiency that he will work with when properly trained will amaze you. This is the type of dog that craves discipline and mental stimulation. Training is what they need. An untrained Anatolian is a handful, and you don't want to go down that road—not even a little bit.

Expectations for Your Dog and Yourself

When you begin your training journey (it really is a journey), it is important to set clear expectations for your dog and for yourself. If you just want him to be able to sit, stay, come, etc., that's fine, but please understand that the Anatolian is capable of much more than that, and you will have a

Photo Courtesy
of Wendy Gerber and John Gerber

much more peaceful time as an owner if you train your dog to the fullest extent possible.

So, when it comes to setting expectations, make sure that you are realistic. Training your Anatolian won't be like winding a clock and forgetting about it. You're going to need to practice your core principles consistently and throughout your dog's entire life. I've said it before, but these dogs are so independent and so smart that you're going to need to do a lot of work to show them that your commands are commands and not just suggestions.

One of the most difficult aspects when it came to training Theo was learning that fact. Even though Laura and I trained him often, or at least what we thought was often, he still only listened some of the time. It wasn't until we pursued more intimate and personal positive training classes that we came to understand what it really meant to train an Anatolian. We hadn't expected to have to adjust our own attitudes towards training in order to give Theo the training he needed and deserved, but we learned that this was necessary.

Understanding and accepting the expectations you assume by adopting or purchasing an Anatolian Shepherd will be vital to the success your dog will have when it comes to training. You must be willing to accept that training will be an everyday thing, and that consistency is everything. Your dog will look for shortcuts and for ways to get his reward without doing all the work he needs to do, but you need to remain disciplined and not give in to the sad eyes and the cuteness.

Electric Fences

Electric fences are a topic of particular interest to Anatolian owners. Some believe in their efficacy and have had no problems using them, while others have had poor experiences. I'll give you some general guidance as to how to approach this touchy topic. An electric fence can be a physically electric-charged fence in and of itself or in addition to your traditional fence, but the invisible type that can be installed underneath the ground is especially popular among families and owners of smaller properties. A great option is to have an electric fence backing up a physical fence.

As discussed earlier in the book, if your Anatolian is going to be spending any time outdoors, you want to invest in a sturdy fence that is at least six feet tall. These are dogs that will get over a short fence, and they're apt to get themselves into danger and/or trouble. If you have a standard fence already, that's great. If you feel that you would like an electric fence in addition to the basic physical fence, I have heard from owners who have employed this method of containment that say it has worked quite well.

If you have no physical fence and are thinking about an electric fence exclusively, I have heard far more negatives about this strategy than positives. There's no feasible way to make this situation work with an Anatolian. Anatolians are livestock guardian dogs, and I have been forwarded countless stories of owners whose Anatolians have become fixated on something of interest and gone through the electric fence to pursue whatever it was that caught their attention. But that's not the end of your issue. Once the fixation wears off, the Anatolian can't get back into the property due to being unwilling to endure the shock of the electric fence upon reentry.

The bottom line is that I endorse an electric fence in addition to a physical fence. But as a barrier on its own, you're looking for trouble and will probably not have any peace of mind leaving your dog out to work or play when guarded only by an electric fence.

Hiring a Trainer and Attending Classes

Some of you reading this book may have an extensive background in training dogs, and that's wonderful! However, for the vast majority of first-time Anatolian Shepherd owners, I strongly recommend hiring a professional trainer to help you through the process. After Theo finished puppy training classes (we did level I and level II), Laura and I kind of thought that would be enough. We had yet to really see Theo's Anatolian personality come out, nor had we experienced his independent and stubborn side quite yet. Sure, he could sit, leave it, and lie down, but we simply had no idea how to get him to stop barking, go into his crate, lie on his bed on command, or do any other higher-level things that we quickly realized were the difference between an average dog and a highly trained dog. When taking Theo out to the dog park became impossible due to his territorial nature and even taking him anywhere that we might run into another dog became a headache, we knew it was time to find a trainer.

HOW TO FIND THE RIGHT TRAINER

Before I get into the specifics about searching for a trainer, let me tell you a little bit about my experience with finding the right trainer for Laura, Theo, and myself. When Theo started to become increasingly stubborn and began to exhibit defiant behavior, we knew that we needed help from a professional. Theo could do the basic things we had learned in puppy training but was increasingly taking our commands as mere options. Additionally, he was becoming more and more protective over Laura and me, to the point where it was becoming problematic to take him anywhere. If we were in the car and he saw another dog, he would freak out. If we were out on a walk and he saw another dog—same story.

That was something that absolutely perplexed us about him at first. He was socialized! Theo had gone to the dog park, was a frequent mainstay at his puppy play daycare due to our jobs, and yet here we found ourselves, seemingly out of nowhere. Little did we know, this is perfectly normal behavior for Theo's breed!

Photo Courtesy
of Alex Norsworthy

A big piece of finding the right trainer is admitting you need a trainer. You may very well find that your Anatolian is friendly, doesn't bark often, and gets along with everyone when he's a puppy. As soon as you start to sense a difference in behavior, whether it be at six months or very commonly around two years, it is time to find a trainer, if you have not already. Any reluctance by your dog to listen to you the first time, every time, is a sign that you need to take this very important step.

Finding the right trainer for you and your dog is a lot like finding the correct veterinarian. Very rarely are you going to find the perfect person on your first attempt, and you're going to likely need to do some extensive searching before you settle on the right person. The thing about the dog-trainer world is that it's not regulated. I'll tell you up-front that I am in no way knowledgeable enough to give you any type of training advice for your dog. However, I could easily print some nifty business cards and advertise myself as a trainer, and people would be none the wiser.

But you're not going to fall victim to an uncredentialed trainer! You're going to find out what to ask and what to look for when searching for prospective trainers, and you'll find the one that is right for you and your dog.

A FEW QUESTIONS TO ASK

When looking for a trainer, it's important to have some questions ready to ask in order to get a feel for who they are and what their philosophies are.

QUESTION #1: HOW LONG HAVE YOU WORKED WITH DOGS?

This is a great starting point to open the conversation with a prospective trainer. Hearing about their experiences is vital to understanding who they are and opens the door to asking more questions about their philosophies and educational experience. The trainer will likely ask you what your experience is with dogs, so it's only fair that you ask the same.

QUESTION #2: DO YOU HAVE CERTIFICATIONS?

Training an Anatolian Shepherd is a challenge, even for professionals, and you're going to want to ask your trainer what their background is with large breeds in addition to what their certifications are. Some credible authorities that provide certification include the Association of Professional Dog Trainers, Certification Council of Professional Dog Trainers, and The Academy of Dog Trainers.

QUESTION #3: WHAT TYPE OF TRAINING DO YOU PROVIDE?

Trainers can offer a variety of services. Some specialize in personalized training, while others use small group settings. Similarly, some trainers are good with dealing with aggressive dogs, training for agility, search and rescue, and other specialized areas. You want to choose a trainer that has experience training dogs in the areas you want your dog trained in and who is well versed in positive training reinforcements. In fact, the ASDCA only recommends positive training methods. Having a professional police dog trainer sounds great, but if they have no experience in the areas you need your dog trained in, it won't be a good fit.

QUESTION #4: HOW DO YOU REWARD GOOD BEHAVIOR/DEAL WITH BAD BEHAVIOR?

Your trainer should know how to reward dogs with multiple methods because not every dog is food-motivated. See what your trainer has to say about reinforcement methods to gain an understanding of how they approach different situations and if they are versatile in their methods. Similarly, ask your prospective trainer how they deal with bad behaviors. Any trainer that resorts to punishment for poor behavior should immediately be crossed off your list.

WHAT TO EXPECT IN YOUR TRAINING CLASSES

Although every trainer is different and every individual dog and owner's needs are different, there are a few general things I can impart to you in regard to what you should expect. You're going to need to understand that the class is just as much for you as it is for your dog. It will challenge you, and it's going to require you to find a level of self-discipline you may not be accustomed to exercising. Expect to unlearn certain things that you were absolutely sure of as a dog owner—even things you have thought to be true from your previous experiences with other dogs. For example, we learned that allowing dogs to greet each other on a leash spontaneously is a big no with the Anatolian. I touched on how to properly do this earlier, but again, we did not know this before working with a trainer.

Anatolians are so smart and so trainable. You're going to see their independent nature and stubbornness on full display while training, but consistency is key, and you're going to have your patience tested, as will your Anatolian. But when training is done successfully, you will both come out armed with the tools needed to have a happy and (mostly) obedient ASD.

Your dog's success is your success, and you should expect to meet obstacles along the way just as your dog will. But you will get through them together, and both be so much better off for it.

CHAPTER 10
Dealing with Unwanted Behaviors

In the last chapter, we discussed training and how essential it is to have a thriving relationship with your Anatolian. I really cannot stress enough how valuable it is to find a training regimen that works for you and your dog and that you are able to stick with long-term. Having a dog that listens to you, respects you, and gives you minimal reason to worry is worth all the money in the world if you ask me.

Anyone who has owned an ASD understands that no matter what type of dog you've owned in your life, attempting to train an ASD is unlike anything else you will ever experience. The faster you accept that you will have your fair share of unwanted and undesirable behaviors to work through, the quicker you can root them out and move past them.

What is Bad Behavior in Dogs?

There's a difference between bad behavior and behavior we don't like as dog owners. For example, a puppy that poops in the house isn't exhibiting bad behavior. He's a puppy, after all. But once he gets to a stage where he is housebroken and knows better, this behavior is unacceptable and needs to be fixed. In short, bad behavior can be any undesirable behavior exhibited by a dog of a mature enough age to "unlearn" the behavior.

Preventing Problem Behaviors

There's an old saying in sports that the best defense is a good offense. The same holds true here. Your best bet for preventing bad behaviors in your ASD is to go on the offensive and do all that you can to prevent those problems from ever taking form. Puppy-proof your house and your property. This includes securing your trash, fencing in your yard/pool, trimming your grass and bushes, creating spaces for your puppy to remain contained, closing the toilet lid, and unplugging electrical cords.

When your Anatolian is a puppy, make sure you put away your shoes and toys, as well as anything else that the puppy can gnaw on by mistake. Reward his good behavior as much as possible. He'll do more of the good stuff and less of the bad if he knows he'll get heaped with praise and treats for certain actions. Another way to help prevent bad behavior is by providing your puppy with enough exercise to keep him physically and mentally stimulated. And as always, consistency is key and makes all the difference.

Fixing Bad Habits

A quick internet search can pull up entire websites dedicated to explaining what unwanted behaviors are in dogs and how to fix them. I'm going to save you time and touch on the few that I have observed as the most common in the Anatolian Shepherd.

Barking

This is going to be a tough one to eliminate in your Anatolian; in fact, the experts will tell you that's it's likely impossible. You'll need to ask yourself if you can live with this trait, as it comes with the territory. If you can live with it, keeping up with training every day is going to be a necessity. Remember, these dogs are naturally protective, and since they were bred to intimidate potential intruders away from their flock, barking is something you're just not

going to be able to get rid of all the way. Luckily, you can manage the behavior in a few ways. You can choose to ignore the barking. This may help when crate training, as your dog will learn that his barking isn't getting him anywhere. Where it probably won't help is when he's trying to warn you about a potential situation he doesn't like.

Photo Courtesy of Rachel Amov

You can also try to remove the stimulus that is prompting the bark. For example, Theo loves to jump onto our bed and look out the window at the neighborhood. This leads to more

HELPFUL TIP
An Independent Streak

Anatolian Shepherds have a reputation for having an independent streak. Many people believe this is an inherited trait, resulting from this breed's early days as sheepdogs who may have been left to fend for themselves and their flocks for long periods. Independence can be a valuable trait in a dog, but if unchecked, it can lead to issues with possessiveness. Be sure to establish consistent and healthy routines and discipline for your dog at an early age to avoid any such issues.

than a few barks at the passersby, other dogs, a stray leaf, etc. Although he won't always remain quiet even after getting used to a particular kind of stimuli, we can prevent him from being on the bed and thus prevent the barking.

Chewing

Many Anatolians love to chew; it just depends on what they decide they enjoy chewing. You should definitely puppy-proof your house thoroughly, but it's common to miss an item here or there, and your Anatolian will likely let you know you've made a mistake. The first step is to put your personal items away and prevent the dog from gaining access to them.

Another option is to ensure your dog is getting enough mental and physical exercise. Chewing is often a manifestation of boredom when it persists past the teething phase. Lastly, I recommend having plenty of great chewable toys to keep your dog busy and occupied. If you catch your ASD in the act of chewing something that is not a dog toy, create a distraction like a loud noise, then replace the item with something the dog is allowed to chew.

If you're lucky, your Anatolian may not be as fond of chewing as another, but it's imperative to play it safe!

Jumping Up

This is one we struggle with to this day with Theo. We didn't realize it, but we were actually giving Theo such mixed signals about jumping up. We felt like fools when our trainer pointed it out to us! Sometimes we were asking him to jump on us to greet us, and other times we were telling him to stop jumping up when guests walked into the house. Imagine how confusing this is for a dog! In order to stop this behavior, you have to turn away from the dog and ignore him when he is looking to jump up. Act as though he is not there, and your ASD will eventually get the signal that the behavior isn't acceptable. This will take time but is typically effective. You may find that your Anatolian doesn't jump up much at all, and if so, keep it that way!

Digging

Anatolians can be quite fond of digging; in fact, most absolutely love it! Most dogs dig, as it's usually an instinctual habit, but ultimately it's a behavior caused by a few different reasons. Whether it be boredom, too much energy, anxiety or fear, a desire to hide his bone or toy, or wanting to gain access to another area, your Anatolian will likely dig up your lawn at some point. You can give them the hugest space possible that you'll allow digging, and they still may dig up that tiny spot you don't want them to touch.

Photo Courtesy of Cristina Padron

Your best bet is to try to pinpoint the source of the behavior. You will most likely need to work with a trainer to try to fully eliminate this trait, but it's not going to be easy. Having a specified area where your ASD is permitted to dig is the best move. I recommend having a fence that is firmly rooted in the ground, or else your Anatolian will find a way to get underneath if he can't get over it.

Begging

I include begging here because this is a common problem with any type of dog. Usually, the culprit is the dog owner, who either intentionally or unintentionally is encouraging the behavior by rewarding the dog with table scraps. No one—including your dog—is buying the excuse that you're just giving him scraps this one time. Your dog will continue to beg for food if you send the message that he'll eventually get something from you. If your dog has this bad habit, think about putting him in another room or in his crate when you eat. If he behaves the way you would like, give him a special treat for being good after you are finished eating.

Bad behavior is going to pop up at some point in your dog's life. The important part is recognizing the behaviors that are a normal part of your puppy growing up and which behaviors are problematic and need to be put to a stop. Working with a trainer is a big help when dealing with an Anatolian, but no matter what your approach is, consistency will be the difference between truly ending bad behaviors or not.

CHAPTER 11
Nutrition

Laura and I may be a bit obsessive when it comes to feeding Theo. We want him to live the healthiest, longest, and best possible life, and we strive to give him the best possible food to help accomplish those goals. I realize that there are many ways to approach meeting the nutritional needs of your dog, and there cannot be one correct way to do so. I will always advocate for the best interest of the dog. When considering whether to adopt or purchase an animal, you need to do a lot of research (as you clearly can tell by now). Estimating what your food expenses will be throughout the year is a critical part of that research.

If you have a working dog, you want to give him the best fuel possible to keep him healthy and nourished to be able to do the best work possible for you. If you have a companion dog like I do, you want to feed him the best possible food you can afford so that you may spend as many high-quality years together as possible. Anatolians do not overeat, as a general rule, so what they do eat should be high-quality and as nourishing as possible.

Anatolians see their food as fuel, and you will optimize your dog's health by providing nourishing food as opposed to prioritizing large quantities. Throughout this chapter, I will tell you a bit about how Laura and I feed Theo, why, and what nutritional options exist for you and your Anatolian.

The Importance of a Good Diet

It may go without saying, but feeding your dog a healthy and nutritious diet is paramount to his long-term health. A dog's body is not so different from our own. When we eat junk, our bodies are negatively affected, and our mental and physical performances suffer. When dogs are fed junk, the same rules apply. Physical and mental processes slow down, life expectancy shortens, and the probability of ailments skyrockets.

Conversely, a diet that is full of nutritious vitamins, protein, carbohydrates, and essential fats is one that will provide real benefits. A dog that is fed a proper diet will live longer, have better dental health, and will have much higher cognitive functioning, along with a host of other benefits, including a beautiful coat. As a large-breed dog, the Anatolian Shepherd will benefit immensely from your proper attention to his dietary needs.

Anatolian breeders (and others) have been extremely diligent in keeping their dogs away from foods that are not approved by the WSAVA. Grain-free diets and many foods not found on the WSAVA's list have been known to cause dilated cardiomyopathy, which is deadly to your dog.

Choosing a Quality Food

Again, research is paramount. I highly recommend consulting with your veterinarian about what food is best for your dog. Every vet varies in their recommendations, but if you resort to internet searches, you are sure to find conflicting opinions everywhere. Some will say absolutely no grain; others will say grain is good. The same goes for dairy, protein intake, fats, etc. No amount of internet research will lead you to any type of conclusive result or answer to the question of "what should I feed my dog?"

However, one of the most important aspects of choosing a quality food for your dog is figuring out what the best possible food is that you can afford even when money is tight. It's easy to go all out when you first get your pup, but if you end up with great food for the first month and then realize you can't afford it any longer, you're not in a good position. It's better to start off with one type of food and then upgrade than it is to get your puppy accustomed to one type of food and then downgrade. The abrupt switch to lower-quality food can then lead to dietary issues.

It's also important to note what your feelings are about kibble versus a raw diet. Although we do not feed Theo kibble, I can absolutely appreciate why some owners prefer that option. Although I do not feel it is the most nutritionally sound food that I can afford to feed my dog, I am in no position to tell you that there are not nutritious kibble varieties because there certainly are.

The Raw Diet Option

We started out feeding Theo kibble. In fact, I recommend feeding your puppy giant breed or large breed kibble for at least the first six months of his life. This will help ensure that he is receiving the vital nutrition that he needs as he grows. In fact, even the biggest supporters of a raw diet tend to shy away from it for puppies. Once a dog has exited that early puppy stage, you can usually start to try out the raw diet.

Ask your veterinarian's opinion about a raw diet. Some vets advocate for the raw diet while others do not. Dog nutrition is not an exact science, but having a trained professional to help you figure it out is essential to providing your dog with the best possible diet.

Photo Courtesy of Cristina Padron

In Theo's case, as he started to grow, we began looking at other options to fill his nutritional needs. As we researched more and more, we came to the conclusion that we did not want to feed Theo kibble any longer. We didn't and still don't have anything against kibble; we just knew it wasn't right for our dog.

Our trainer and our daycare owner both recommended looking into a raw diet for Theo, and we felt like it could be a possibility. Instead of jumping right into it, we consulted with our veterinarian, who backed the idea and said that she felt like it was a tremendous option for Theo's breed, size, and genetic makeup. An even more specialized professional to discuss the raw diet with would be a veterinary nutritionist who can speak at lengths about the pros and cons and the overall transitional process if you believe it is the right option for your dog!

Luckily for us, we have access to a farm nearby that

FUN FACT
Largest Dog in the UK

An Anatolian Shepherd named Kurt was a contender for the title of largest dog in the UK in 2016. Kurt measures seven ft tall when he stands on his rear legs and measures 40 inches from paw to shoulder. Weighing in at 11 stone, or 154 pounds, Kurt is actually smaller than the UK's largest dog, a Great Dane named Freddy. Kurt's owner, Tracy, says: "He's the most loving, sloppy, adorable lump, and has no idea of his size and will just lie all over you and flatten you." This large dog eats $138 of food each month!

specializes in producing raw food for dogs. The food we have access to has no bones and has all the necessary probiotics and essential vitamins that Theo needs. That is a key detail that cannot be overlooked. Feeding your dog a proper raw/homecooked diet is not as simple as giving him hamburger meat and calling it a day. It is going to take research and education as well as understanding your dog's dietary needs. You're going to need to also provide him with sufficient sources of calcium, phosphorous, carbohydrates, and omega-3s, etc. Again, conferring with a veterinary nutritionist is a great idea if you are even slightly unsure of what to do with food!

Now, there is also research detailing the risks associated with a raw diet. These risks are often tied to the original idea proposed in 1993 by Australian veterinarian Ian Billinghurst. Raw meat can be a source of contamination and bacterial infections for dogs and humans. Eating a strictly raw diet can leave dogs lacking in various nutritional areas that are essential to their health. However, studies have been conducted pointing to the presence of bacteria such as E. coli in commercially produced food as well.

The overall point here is that there are pros and cons to whatever you decide to feed your Anatolian. The essential thing to remember is to purchase within your means while considering the food sources that will provide your dog with the essential nutrition that he requires to function at optimal levels.

Supplements

If you are unsure if your Anatolian is receiving everything he needs from his diet alone, using certain supplements to provide him with essential nutrition may be a good idea. Some great supplements include:

- Multivitamins
- Hip and Joint Supplements
- Advanced Joint Supplements for Large Breed Dogs
- Cosequin DS Plus MSM Maximum Strength Chewable Tablets.

I recommend getting those supplements in soft chew form. One other supplement Laura and I swear by is Dr. Marty PROPOWER PLUS, which is a probiotic blend designed to improve gut health.

Treats and People Food

You will be giving your dog plenty of treats throughout his puppy stages and adulthood. Besides working as a great motivational tool, treats like bones and a peanut-butter-filled Kong are a great way to stimulate your dog and occupy him as well. However, ensure that there is no xylitol in the ingredients of the peanut butter in your house, as it is known to be deadly to dogs.

Not all treats are created equal, of course, and you will want to look out for a few things on the label to steer clear of. Artificial colors, sweeteners, salt, syrups, and meat by-products are all no-nos for feeding your dog. You want to mainly purchase treats made with whole meats, fruits, veggies, and grains. If your dog has an allergy, check with your veterinarian, who will be able to do allergy testing.

TABLE SCRAPS

When it comes to feeding your dog table scraps, it's very difficult not to give in to those sad eyes and drool, but you must. Here are three great rules of thumb to follow when it comes to table scraps.

RULE #1 – NO TABLE SCRAPS!

Don't give in to the cuteness. Anatolians are notorious for their sad eyes and persistence, even as puppies. Once you begin to reward your dog for begging at the table, the game is over. He has won. You have lost. You've just taught the dog that this behavior is acceptable.

RULE #2 – YOUR DOG IS NOT YOUR VACUUM CLEANER

Am I guilty of this one? If I'm honest, yeah, I am, at times. But what I have seen repeatedly in my life are owners who constantly allow their dog to eat anything that has fallen onto the ground at dinner or while cooking. This is not a good habit to allow your dog to form unless you want a sous chef following you everywhere you go or a dinner guest with drool hanging out of his mouth.

RULE #3 – KNOW WHAT YOU CAN AND CANNOT FEED YOUR DOG

I don't think I need to bend your ear for hours about what is and isn't acceptable to give your dog, but it does amaze me to find that many people are still uninformed about the many foods that can make dogs sick or even kill them. Stay far away from grapes, onions, garlic, and chocolate, as those are the big-ticket items that are most notorious for causing illnesses in canines. Even small amounts of these foods can kill your dog—even if it's just one time! However, certain other items are to be avoided as well, including almonds, macadamia nuts, and ice cream. In general, dairy can be acceptable for dogs (just stay away from ice cream due to high dairy and sugar content) in small to moderate quantities, but it is best to avoid giving your dog large quantities as it can be difficult for canines to digest dairy.

Weight Management

The Anatolian Shepherd is not a dog known for overeating. In fact, you may very well find that your ASD might appear not to be interested in his food at times. Laura and I had that experience with Theo where he was not eating his kibble as a puppy, and we simply didn't know what to do to get him to eat. That's when we started exploring other options and came to the raw diet/home-cooked diet as an option.

If you think your dog is underweight, ask your vet's opinion. If they believe your dog needs to gain weight, ask for recommendations as to how to go about this. Laura and I first started using broth as a way to entice Theo to eat all of his kibble at mealtime. This worked wonders at first, but after a week or two, he resorted back to not being interested. Since we've moved to a holistic raw diet, he eats everything and licks the bowl clean.

If an Anatolian becomes overweight, their organs and joints can have an incredible toll placed upon them. While some are very active dogs, others can be pretty content to remain inactive. It is going to depend on the dog. Seek veterinarian advice if you are unsure if your dog is overweight or eating too much.

CHAPTER 12

Health and Your Anatolian Shepherd

Taking care of a dog is a big responsibility. Taking care of a big dog is a massive responsibility. Your Anatolian is going to go from being a large puppy to a large adult in what will, unfortunately, feel like the blink of an eye. It's important to make note of the best ways you can support your dog and ensure that he lives the healthiest and overall highest-quality life possible.

One of the first things Laura and I did with Theo was figure out the best ways we could care for him throughout his various stages of development. Keeping an Anatolian's specific health needs in mind is critical in providing the proper care for your pup throughout his entire life.

Like many dogs, many of the conditions that could potentially afflict your Anatolian are genetically passed down from his parents. One of the reasons for asking your breeder questions about the sire and dam is to get a sense of any red flags or potential health concerns awaiting down the road. While a health concern could arise that no one saw coming, preparing yourself for the most common ailments and educating yourself about them will help ensure that you can provide your pup with the attention and care that he deserves.

HELPFUL TIP
Recognizing Osteochondritis Dissecans (OCD)

Anatolian Shepherds can be more likely to develop orthopedic problems compared to smaller dog breeds. One of these diseases is called osteochondritis dissecans (OCD) and can affect the knee, ankle, and/or spine. Signs of this disease include limping, difficulty walking, change in gait, or difficulty rising. Diagnosis is made by X-rays or CT scans, and treatment may involve surgery or pain-management techniques assigned by your veterinarian.

Common Health Concerns

So, here are some common health concerns and ailments that you may experience with your Anatolian Shepherd.

Infections

While not a breed-specific condition, keep in mind that Anatolians are just as susceptible to bacterial and viral infections as any other dog. Infections like rabies and distemper can be prevented through vaccination, however.

Weight Concerns

While it is generally accepted that the Anatolian Shepherd will not over-eat, any dog will be tempted to eat your leftover food and too many treats if you allow it to do so. Anatolians have some of the biggest puppy dog eyes you can imagine, and it's going to take a serious amount of self-discipline to just say no, but remember that you want your pup to live a long, healthy life with you. Giving table scraps and constant treats is not the way that you will achieve that!

Photo Courtesy
of Krista Young

Parasites

Again, like any other dog, Anatolians are vulnerable to ticks, ear mites, worms, and all other types of undesirable creatures. Make sure that your Anatolian is not able to drink any unclean water, which may be difficult if he is outside working for long stretches of the day, but it is still important to remain diligent about this. Also, ensure that your dog is not being bitten by mosquitos, and if he is, seek care and treatment as soon as possible. Mosquitos can carry heartworm, which is a type of parasitic roundworm. Heartworm may lead to various organ diseases and death! Dogs can also potentially spread parasites to you and your family, as well.

Genetic Issues

Due to the size and stature of the Anatolian Shepherd, the risk of developing bloat (the torsion of the stomach and subsequent filling with gas) exists, as it would with any other dog. Torsion will cut off the blood supply to the stomach and spleen and can lead to a quick death. Signs of bloat may include heaving or retching from your dog. There have been instances where people have had their dogs go under the knife to preventatively tack their stomach down, but this is not common for the ASD and is more commonly done during the spay and neutering process in other dog breeds. Consult your vet for any advice in that department. If you suspect your pup has bloat, head to the emergency vet right away.

Hip and Elbow Dysplasia

Like any big dog, the Anatolian is at-risk for hip and elbow dysplasia, although the risks are lessened due to years of selective breeding by responsible breeders who health test these two areas. These two diseases are genetically inherited and can cause the hip and elbow joints to develop in ways that will result in dysplasia. If you notice your dog having difficulty getting himself up from the ground or his back legs seem to be weak, confer with your vet about the next steps. A vet may suggest surgery and/or other treatments to limit the effects of dysplasia.

Allergies

When looking out for allergies in your ASD, keep in mind that they manifest differently than in humans. Where you and I might get a runny nose and sneeze, dogs get itchy skin. If you catch your pup gnawing at his paws or notice redness on his stomach, ears, or on any "folds" of skin, confer with your vet for treatment options.

Hypothyroidism

Hyperthyroidism involves the body not making enough thyroid hormone, and your dog can exhibit this in having a dry coat, hair loss, change in behavior, and, possibly, weight gain. The most common treatment that a vet will prescribe is a pill that will help with hormone production.

Bone Cancer

As your Anatolian gets older, he may be more liable to develop osteosarcoma, a form of bone cancer. While Anatolians are known to be healthier than most other large and giant breed dogs, this type of bone cancer is more common in these breeds. If you notice a limp or lameness in your dog, do not waste any time in getting your pup examined.

Photo Courtesy of Ashley Clement

Spaying/Neutering

Spaying or neutering is often the best choice for the vast majority of dog owners. There is quite a bit of disagreement about the best time to do this, with some arguing that it should be done as soon as possible, while others believe in waiting until the dog is between 18-24 months to allow for proper bone development and the utilization of hormones. Just like with other important health-related decisions, discuss this with your vet. Keep in mind that vets may err on the side of sooner as a means of population control, but that this does not always mean that it is best for the dog. Take what your breeder has to say seriously, as they will have a lot to advise in this department. Spaying or neutering will also provide the vet and you with any type of information about how your dog reacts to anesthesia. There is also the option of purchasing pre-anesthesia bloodwork and during surgery monitoring.

Pet Insurance

Something you should do right away is purchase a pet insurance policy for your Anatolian. A pet insurance policy is going to work similarly to a health insurance policy for a person. You can choose specific coverages, and certain policies are geared more towards large-breed dogs, but basically, a pet insurance policy is going to cover any number of conditions. One of the most popular types of policies is an accident and illness plan which will cover certain diseases, like cancer, allergies, infections, and similar ailments. Other policy options will cover unfortunate events, such as if your pet is struck by a car, tears a ligament, or if they ingest something poisonous or otherwise harmful. We have ours through Nationwide, and it costs about $48 per month but could be less. We purchased a higher tier to cover certain surgeries that can be more common for big dogs to give us a sense of relief and security if Theo ever has an unexpected ailment. For us, paying for a pet insurance policy is worth every single penny.

Taking Care of Your Anatolian

You now have a good idea of what you could expect to be dealing with one day. Of course, the above is not an exhaustive list, nor is this a list designed to make you worry over every little thing your dog does. However, being prepared will provide you with peace of mind at the end of the day.

Taking care of your Anatolian requires a good deal of common sense and falls in line with the rules that healthy people follow. A good diet, plenty of exercise, dental hygiene (brushing every day is best), and overall hygiene are huge parts of keeping your dog safe and healthy. Make sure that you are staying up to date on checkups, vaccinations, and other routine healthcare procedures.

CHAPTER 13
You and Your Senior

> *ASDs want to keep working; it is the essence of their being. Don't retire them to the house, instead reduce the area they have to cover and prevent them from running on rough ground or hard surfaces.*
>
> ### NANCY BURNS
> *Marble Peaks Ranch*

While Theo is just shy of three as I write this, I know that he is going to one day be a senior, and my wife and I will need to provide the same standard of care for him then as we do now. After all, your pup is only part of your life, but you are his entire life. While dogs don't get to stick around for your entire life, you'll be there for every part of theirs. Even though your senior dog might not be able to move with the same precision or get up quite as fast when he hears a noise outside the door, he'll always be there to protect you and will be by your side, even if he falls asleep a bit often.

In general, Anatolians live somewhere in the low to mid-teens in human years. Just like people, Anatolians vary greatly in this respect.

It's important to take a few things into consideration when you think about caring for your senior dog. Let's take a look.

How Old Is Old?

There's a bit of debate about how different dogs age, and truthfully, all dogs age a bit differently. In general, six to eight can be considered senior status for your Anatolian—or middle-aged at the least.

Photo Courtesy
of Rachel Amov

What to Look For

As your dog ages, there are some general signs you can look out for to get a sense of where he is in his life cycle.

CHANGES IN MUSCULAR STRUCTURE AND STRENGTH

Atrophy is a common sign of aging in all animals and humans. You will notice that as your Anatolian ages, his legs or even head may lose some mass, and he may run with a bit less power. This can be tricky because dogs exhibit pain in very different ways than humans, and not all dogs exhibit pain in the same ways.

Ensure that you always provide your dog with exercise, even as he ages. It may seem at times like it is hard work for your senior pup, but exercise is the best thing for an aging dog. He needs it just as much now as he did when he was young! If you notice a significant loss of mass in areas like the belly, contact your vet, as this could be a sign of something seriously wrong.

LOWER AND SLOWER

As your Anatolian gets older, he may spend more time in low places like on the floor as opposed to the couch or on the ground floor of your home versus upstairs. Keep in mind that as your dog gets older, stairs may become more difficult for him to walk up. Take note of any joint and muscle stiffness. Sometimes rainy and cold weather can have an adverse effect on arthritis, which is common in dogs as they age. Medication may help alleviate any joint pain related to arthritis, but you should still consistently monitor your dog's condition to ensure it isn't deteriorating. Hypothyroidism could also be a cause of slowing down in your dog, so if you have any suspicion that your dog may be experiencing this condition, consult your vet as this is a very easy condition to treat, as we noted in the last chapter.

If your senior Anatolian is experiencing either weight gain or loss, it may indicate disease, which your vet can help to rule out, or it could suggest your dog's diet needs to be adjusted to match his "new" old body and metabolism. Getting a senior dog blood work-up is also a good idea here. Older dogs might be more prone to weaker bladders and have accidents similar to when they were puppies, or they might experience constipation.

In general, be flexible with your old pup as he ages. Make sure that he has accessible and comfortable bedding that will be easy on his joints. Don't have expectations of your old pup that may have been fair when he was half his age. Your senior dog may not be exactly the way he was when he was younger, but he'll always give you everything he's got. He deserves the same.

Regular Vet Visits

Just because your dog is a bit older doesn't mean you should skimp on your vet visits! When your pup gets a bit older, make sure you are taking them to the vet at least once a year for a full examination. Many ailments may be hidden from physical sight, and a blood panel and other tests can help uncover any potential concerns. Make sure you ask your vet plenty of questions! Ask if their weight is still on target for their age and if there are any supplements you could or should be giving to them. It is also useful to have your vet give you tips or pointers on how to evaluate your pup at home for more obvious conditions like weakened joints, cataracts, or hearing loss.

Supplies

As your Anatolian ages, you should ask your vet for any products they'd recommend to strengthen their joints. Usually, a glucosamine supplement is advisable to help fortify their joints as they age, but other changes or additions to your dog's diet may also be advisable. Continue to give your pup toys that they enjoy playing with and bones or other chew toys they enjoy, as dental health remains important, even in these elder years! Your dog may require some softer bedding that will be easier on their joints, too.

Mental and Physical Exercise for the Aging Anatolian

It might seem like your Anatolian wants to exercise less and less as they age, but as their owner, and as the one who knows better, it's vital that you keep them active both mentally and physically. Remember that these dogs were bred to work! Anatolians need and even crave mental stimulation, and this doesn't change for your old boy! Even if they never worked with livestock, or if you've scaled back or even eliminated all of their farm responsibilities, find ways to keep them cognitively engaged. Play hide and seek games with their favorite toys or even be the object that is hiding! You could also play the old "hide the treat under the cup" game and have your dog try to figure out which cup the treat is underneath by knocking them down. Using food and toys to come up with creative games to give your Anatolian's brain the stimulation it needs is essential to keeping them sharp and living a meaningful life with you for as long as possible. Brain games that get them cognitively focused are also a good idea, even though Anatolians are not the most playful of dogs.

Physically, your Anatolian isn't going to want to do many of the physical things that they used to, and that's fine. But you should still be taking them on intentional walks. What I mean is that if you just let your pup out in the yard to roam around and run on their own, their natural desire to do so is going to

HELPFUL TIP
Sensitivity to Anesthesia

Anatolian Shepherds are extremely sensitive to anesthesia. Many dogs from this breed require only a tenth of the normal dosage of anesthetic. It's recommended that veterinarians begin with this reduced dosage and increase in small increments until the dosage is sufficient.

wain as they age. By taking them for walks on their leash and controlling the length and intensity of the walk, you are ensuring that your Anatolian is exercising a proper amount. These walks don't have to be for miles at a time, but a ten to fifteen-minute walk two or three times a day should do the trick.

Dealing with Changes

As your dog ages, you may notice that they don't act entirely the same. Senior dogs are more likely to develop blindness, incontinence, and experience hearing loss. It is best to confer with your vet about what to do when you notice that your dog is losing their sight, having accidents, or not responding to your voice or noises that they used to.

BLINDNESS

If your pup has lost their vision or is losing their vision, there are things that you can do to lend a hand to them and make their life easier. Watch your puppy when they're young, and you'll notice that they allow their nose to guide them most of the time. Well, turn this strength into an even greater strength by using their keen sense of smell to guide them when on walks or around the house. Make sure that you are helping your pup out by eliminating any harmful objects that they could stumble into. Ensure that you are still actively exercising their brain and body, too. Blindness may be tough on both of you, but it's not a reason to give up on making more great memories with your Anatolian.

DEAFNESS

Anatolians have selective hearing their entire life, so having an older Anatolian who has lost his hearing might not be as difficult as it could be for other dog owners! To help with managing your senior with hearing loss, you can develop hand signals or other ways to communicate with them that allow them to use visual cues. Make sure you don't startle your pup in situations where hearing would normally alert them of your presence. Having your Anatolian wear a little tag that tells strangers that they are deaf will also be helpful.

DEAFNESS AND BLINDNESS

This is a tough situation to see your once youthful pup deal with, but it can certainly happen. Luckily, they still have three great senses left to help them get around! Utilize them as much as possible! Provide scent trails to lead your dog around and use taste and touch as much as possible, too. Your pup needs to continue to feel comfortable in his home, and knowing that you are still there and actively taking care of him is going to do wonders for his continued mental and physical well-being.

Their dog losing sight or hearing is a scary prospect for dog owners, but there are so many great things we can do to help maximize the senses our Anatolians still have. It's best to retire your dog from his farm work or figure out what jobs that he can do successfully that won't put him or any other animals in danger.

INCONTINENCE

If you notice your pal is having accidents, take him to the vet to have tests done to rule out any potential cancers or other dangerous ailments. Incontinence can happen from spaying but can also be because of some type of pain. Only your vet will have the ability to diagnose any serious health conditions at the root of your dog's incontinence, but incontinence is not always a sign of a health condition. As your Anatolian ages, he will lose muscle around the pelvic region, which can inevitably result in more accidents. Again, do not panic if you notice your dog having accidents. While serious diseases or ailments could be behind this, there are also normal reasons related to aging to consider, as well.

What to Look for If You Suspect the Worst

Unfortunately, sometimes your worst-case scenario comes to life. If you begin to suspect that your pup is in too much pain to continue on your journey, you should first look for certain things and ask yourself certain questions before making that tough decision. Things to look out for include if your dog has lost their desire to eat or drink. This can be a sign that there is something wrong with your dog, and you should consult your vet immediately as you may need to adjust the diet or method for feeding. Other signs to look out for:

- Your dog's behavior has changed, and they've become irritable, tired, aggressive, or experienced some other drastic shift from their usual personality.

- Is your dog vocalizing more often? This could include yips or whines, or other indications of pain.

- How is their demeanor? Are they tired, depressed, or anxious? Anxiety can indicate dementia or canine cognitive dysfunction in your pup.

- Are there any other signs that your dog might be in some type of physical pain? Are they limping, hobbling, unable to stand up easily, or can only walk for short distances?

You will know your Anatolian's usual behavior patterns better than anyone. If you suspect that something has changed and is giving you cause for concern, call your vet and seek attention immediately. It's always better to be proactive than reactive.

Euthanasia

Before even considering euthanasia, evaluate your dog's quality of life. Although this area is common sense to many people, considering what your dog is able to do day to day, what type of pain they may be in, and their overall health is critical prior to taking this massive leap. Commonly referred to as being "put to sleep," euthanasia is a very humane and painless way to end your Anatolian's pain at the end of their life. The process can typically be conducted at your house or at the veterinarian's office and usually costs between $50 and $100. Remember, your job as your Anatolian's protector is to comfort them, and if there was ever a time, this is it. Sit with them and hold them, pet them, tell them how much you love them.

Your vet may administer a sedative, or they might not; it will depend on your pup's condition. The most common drug used for the euthanasia process will be the drug pentobarbital, which is a seizure medication that is usually given via IV in one of the dog's legs. The drug will effectively slow the dog's heart and brain functions to a stop in a minute or two. Your dog may let out a last breath, empty their bladder, and their eyes may not close, but the important thing here is to be prepared for all of these things. Also, understand that one or none of these may happen. Your dog has experienced no pain throughout the process.

MULTIDOG HOUSEHOLDS

It may be best for you to opt to have your dog put to sleep at home if you have other dogs or animals in your care. This is especially true with dogs, as they will grow confused and search for their deceased friend if they do not know what happened to them. If you have children at home, you may not want to put them in a position to see this happen, however. Whatever works best for your family in this delicate situation is the correct path to take.

WHAT TO DO NEXT

Remember, your Anatolian shared their entire life with you and loved you with every part of their being. However you choose to part with them is your decision, but it should always be done with your dog's best interest in mind. You may wish to bury them at a pet cemetery or have them cremated. Vets will typically have a few services they work with to recommend for either option. No matter what you choose, treating your best friend with the care and love they deserve in their last moments is the thing that matters most.

WHEN THE TIME COMES

Every great story must come to an end, and boy, your story with your Anatolian will have been one for the books. If you're anything like me, you don't think about this day. I'll be honest with you: there's no way to emotionally prepare for this moment. It's going to hurt. You're going to miss your pup. But think of all the time you spent together and all of the love you will always have for him. You loved each other for better and for worse, but time always catches up. Even though we can't possibly prepare our hearts for this, you owe it to your Anatolian to keep him from hurting in the end.

If you suspect that your dog is ill and your vet advises you to do what's best for your pup, consider the advice seriously. The selfish part of us wants to deny it, and maybe getting a second opinion wouldn't hurt. But when you can look in your dog's eyes, sometimes you can just see that the time has come.

If you have children, be honest and open with them about what is happening, but make sure it is age-appropriate. It's going to be a painful time for everyone involved, but if you think about it as one final act of compassion and love for your best friend, it may be a little bit easier.

CHAPTER 14

What Makes the Anatolian Truly Special

There is no other dog like the Anatolian Shepherd. There are other livestock guardian dogs and other large breeds that I find to be amazing, too, but until you come to own an Anatolian, you'll never know the utter joy of having one to call your lifelong companion. Besides the fact that they are the most loyal creatures in the world, and aside from the fact that your dog will drive you a bit crazy here and there, I am confident that you'll fall in love with this absolutely special breed.

I've walked you through all of the information I wish I had really known prior to adopting Theo. Everything to this point has been geared toward allowing you to be the best owner and companion possible for your ASD. But it's also useful to hear some of the wonderful things that you can expect as an owner of an Anatolian Shepherd.

A Lifelong Guardian and a Best Friend

If your dog is working with livestock, he has a flock to be mindful of and to protect at all costs. If your dog is your companion, he may very well treat you like one of his flock. While many dogs are protective of their owners, the Anatolian is going to be perhaps the most loyal and protective dog you could ever imagine. When Theo got to be around six months, I've described to you how his demeanor shifted to a much more dominant mentality, and training became necessary.

While all of that is certainly true, that shift in behavior also marked the start of something special. It became clear that Theo was now viewing himself as our protector. We had to be careful to train him so that he did not exhibit aggressive tendencies toward unfamiliar people and situations, but keep in mind that Anatolians will always be independent thinkers. But seeing

Theo grow into a large, strong, guardian-like dog can only be described as pure amazement. As an Anatolian owner, you'll feel that genuine love that your dog has for you, and you'll see that look he gets that tells you he would do anything to make sure that you are safe.

Intelligence

Throughout this book, I've stated that the Anatolian Shepherd is one of the smartest dogs you will ever encounter. They are able to pick up on things going on around them with such precision and quickness that it's like you've got another human living in the house. When Theo started to mature, we noticed this intelligence almost right away. Theo realized what the sliding door lock looked like when it was unlocked, and when he noticed it wasn't locked, he'd help himself to a relaxing seat on the patio. But when he saw that the lock was in position, he would never bother to head over to the door.

The same goes for the Anatolian's ability to train you as their owner. While any dog has an uncanny ability to get what it wants, I promise you that

Anatolians will try to outsmart you every step of the way. While it's a learning curve for most, Laura and I have turned Theo's little behaviors into learning experiences and adjusted our behaviors along the way.

The Anatolian Shepherd will hide things from you that he knows he's not supposed to have and behave in a super stealth-like manner when he's in the middle of shredding something or gnawing on something forbidden. If you own one for long enough, you'll find out exactly what I mean when you can't see all of your dog but can see enough to know he's got something clutched between his two giants paws that he's enjoying ever so silently.

Having a dog that is so intelligent is certainly hard work at times, but when you're asking him to work and to guide other animals (after all, that's why they were bred), it's obvious that thousands of years of conditioning have paid off in the breed's characteristics.

It Feels Like You're in On a Secret

Prior to getting Theo, and even after bringing him home, we had no idea what an Anatolian Shepherd was. When we realized that we did indeed have an Anatolian Shepherd, we did everything we could to learn about the breed and how to best raise one. Now, it feels like we have our own little secret thing going with our "big man," as we call him. Living in New York, I've never seen another Anatolian Shepherd around my area. That's not to suggest that there aren't any, but I would be willing to bet that seeing another Anatolian isn't a very common occurrence for most. There are certain geographic areas that are far more likely to have Anatolians due to work demands, but in general, you're going to be the owner of an uncommon breed.

Looking back on everything, it's quite funny to think about all the different suggestions that strangers, friends, and family gave me and Laura about what type of dog Theo might be. We sure did hear it all those first few months. You would have thought we had the funkiest looking canine ever if you heard some of the suggestions we got—Pitbull, Collie, German Shepherd, Great Pyrenees; someone even suggested some type of hound mix. Crazy! But we always welcomed the input because it meant that people were taking an interest in our puppy! But once we zeroed in on Theo's exact breed and learned all about the Anatolian Shepherd, we couldn't have been more proud to own this type of dog, which brings me to my point.

People are going to be curious about your dog.

It's just a fact! The Anatolian was only brought here a few decades ago, as we noted in the opening chapter, and it's still a relatively uncommon breed to see. While more and more people have seen the value of keeping an Anatolian as a companion, you will still find yourself in the minority in regard to owning one. If you're anything like me, you'll take pride in owning a living, breathing, adorable, stubborn conversation starter. Of course, don't get an Anatolian because you're seeking attention. I've covered enough points about why you need to be absolutely certain you must have an Anatolian before adopting or seeking out a breeder. But as a reminder, do not seek out this dog, or any dog, for selfish reasons.

The Community Is Special

Laura and I immediately searched for Facebook Groups and internet websites where we could connect with other Anatolian Shepherd owners. We felt a huge relief when we were able to find a few that were run by very professional administrators who truly care and love the Anatolian Shepherd.

That's something I want to make a special note of, too. This dog was protected for hundreds, if not thousands of years by Turkish farmers that wanted to ensure that the Anatolian stayed in their region. They knew exactly how special this working dog was, and they didn't want anything to devalue or impurify the breed. When the dog was brought to the United States, it was done with such care and attention as to truly honor the breed. The leaders of these Anatolian Shepherd communities devote their efforts to making sure that these dogs are protected, honored, and understood.

The fact that so many Anatolian owners care so deeply about this breed speaks to how large of an impact the dogs can have on your life. Laura and I agree that the Anatolian Shepherd community is completely one of a kind. It's really something special to be a part of, and we wouldn't trade that for the world. I really can't promote connecting with your fellow Anatolian owners enough. Your most valuable resource will really be your inner community of Anatolian owners.

Parting Words

Welcome to the family, and boy, do I mean it when I say that this is a family. Owning and raising an Anatolian Shepherd is going to be some of the best and hardest work that you will ever do. But it's going to be the best days of your life that you get to spend together. Theo has been both the most challenging and the most rewarding part of my adult life. As a puppy, he was like a lump of clay, waiting to be molded into whatever shape my wife and I wanted to turn him into. As he got older, we realized that he had

Photo Courtesy of Heidi Krol Stonecoat Farm Anatolians

always known what shape he was turning into and was simply letting us have our fun.

You are embarking on what will be the best years of your life. It does not matter whether you're raising a true livestock guardian dog or a companion; you will both go through so many of the same trials, triumphs, and struggles whether your Anatolian does any outside labor or not.

Theo would want me to make sure that you know that no matter how many times an Anatolian might not listen, he'll always love and protect you with every part of his being. Whether it's an eight-foot grizzly or a leaf that has gone rogue, he'll always be between you and them. That's the beauty of the Anatolian Shepherd. He's a livestock guardian dog, and you'll always be the most important member of his flock.

CPSIA information can be obtained
at www.ICGtesting.com
Printed in the USA
LVHW070828090622
720764LV00002BA/14

9 781954 288232